To Rou
who is always
on my mind
Happy Birthday!

Adam   14/3/2015

Adam Yamey, born in London in 1952, is a dental surgeon by profession. He enjoys travelling, and has published two historical novels, "Aliwal" (2010) & "Rogue of Rouxville" (2012). He is married and has one child, a daughter.

Copyright © Adam R Yamey, 2012

The moral right of the author has been asserted.

The characters mentioned in the description of the author's trip to Albania actually existed, but their names have been changed to protect their privacy.

All rights reserved.

No part of this publication may be reproduced, stored in a retrieval system, or transmitted, in any form or by any other means without the written permission of the author, nor be otherwise circulated in any form of binding or cover other than that which it is published and without a similar condition being imposed on the subsequent publisher.

ISBN 978-1-291-11147-7

http://www.adamyamey.com

Albania

On My

Mind

Adam Yamey

"It struck me that Albania was the sort of place that might keep a man from yawning"

[John Buchan, 1915]

In loving memory of Robert and Margaret Harkness

Albanian costumes, 1957

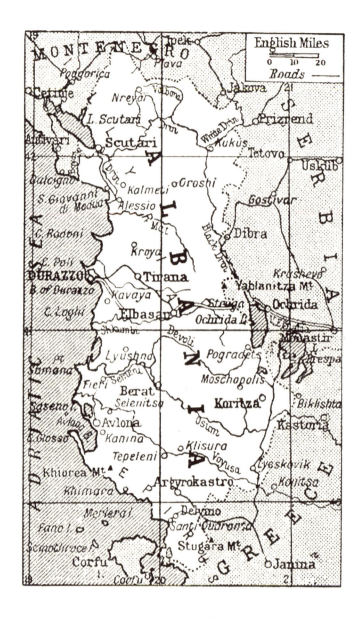

Albania in 1922

[Scutari= Shkodër, Durazzo= Durrës, Pogradets=Pogradec, Santi Quaranta= Sarandë,

Kroya= Krujë, Koritza= Korçë, and Podgorica= Titograd]

A simplified chronology of modern Albanian history

1405: Birth of George Kastrioti Skanderbeg: the Albanian leader, who kept the Ottomans at bay for more than 20 years.

1410: Birth of Lekë Dukagjini: Prince of the Albanians, and lawmaker.

1478: Albania becomes part of the Ottoman Empire.

1908: Birth of Enver Hoxha.

1913: The Conference of London declares Albania to be an independent state.

1928: The dictator, Ahmed Zogu, declares himself king ('King Zog') of Albania.

1939: Mussolini invades Albania.

1943: Hitler invades Albania

1945: End of the Second World War. Albania is the only country in mainland Europe to have a larger Jewish population in 1945 than in 1939. Enver Hoxha and his Communist supporters begin their long rule of the country.

1947: Albania falls out with its communist neighbour Yugoslavia.

1956: Albania divorces itself from the USSR, its ally since 1945.

1978: Albania cuts ties with the People's Republic of China, which had become the country's chief political ally after the USSR had fallen from Hoxha's favour.

1981: Mehmet Shehu, Hoxha's right hand man and likely successor 'commits suicide'.

1984: Adam Yamey visits Albania.

1985: Enver Hoxha dies. He is succeeded by Ramiz Alia.

1991: Democratic choice of government introduced to Albania.

Women dancing, 1909

"Anon from the castle walls
The crescent banner falls,
And the crowd beholds instead,
Like a portent in the sky,
Iskander's banner fly,
The Black Eagle with double head;
And a shout ascends on high,
For men's souls are tired of the Turks,
And their wicked ways and works,
That have made of Ak-Hissar
A city of the plague;
And the loud, exultant cry
That echoes wide and far
Is: "Long live Scanderbeg!"

[From *Tales of a Wayside Inn*,
Henry Wadsworth Longfellow, 1863]

ALBANIA ON MY MIND

History of an obsession

Until early in the 1990s, Albania, the small state on the western side of the Balkan peninsular, was at least as tightly sealed-off from the eyes of the outside world as is North Korea today. It was a maverick socialist state, which, under the leadership of its dictator Enver Hoxha, regarded first the USSR and then later the People's Republic of China, as being too reactionary to be its allies. Few visited it, the only country in Europe where Stalin was publicly revered long after his death, and even fewer escaped from it. And, not many people shared my long fascination with the country.

I was 7 or 8 years old, and knew nothing about Albania or the Balkans, when my father came home one evening and presented me with a copy of the *"Crab with the Golden Claws"*. That gift began my love of the adventures of Tintin, a series of comic books written and illustrated by the Belgian Georges Hergé. Gradually, I acquired the whole of the collection of these superbly drawn cartoon books, which chronicled the exciting deeds of Tintin, the reporter who is easily recognised by the tuft of hair springing out above his forehead and the little white dog called 'Snowy' that accompanies him all over the world and beyond. They visit North and South America, Africa, Europe, Asia, and even the moon. The stories that attracted me most were those set in the imaginary countries of Borduria and Syldavia. The former was Hergé's representation of a Central European state, and the latter of a Balkan state. I believe that it was the pictures that he drew of these two imaginary countries that triggered my interest in the Balkans. To this day, I cannot explain why it was Hergé's pictures of this region rather than of any of the far more exotic places, which he depicted in his stories, that captured my imagination, but that is what happened.

My curiosity about the Balkans was enhanced by the fact that when I was a child they were communist countries behind the so-called 'Iron Curtain'. My parents refused to have anything to do with countries under the rule of governments that had not been elected in free elections. Thus, they were reluctant to travel to Spain, Portugal, their native South Africa (this did have a freely elected government, but the voters were not representative of the whole population), or any of the 'Iron Curtain' countries. So strong was my parents' desire not to support the totalitarian regimes, that my father preferred to buy pickled gherkins that had been produced in Holland or West Germany rather than in, for example, Hungary or Poland. That the Balkan countries were considered to be 'forbidden fruit' by my parents, further increased my interest in them.

Whilst most of my school friends were 'exploring' girls, attending parties, experimenting with marijuana, cigarettes, and alcohol, I spent much of my spare time during my mid-teens haunting second-hand bookshops.

In the second half of the 1960s, Hampstead Village, which was in easy walking distance of my family home, had at least 5 such establishments. My favourite store, and one of the most reasonable, was located in Perrin's Lane. It was run by a scholarly old man. He sat reading in his untidy shop, surrounded by books, which were scattered disorderly on every available surface including the floor. Every now and then, he used to burst out laughing and would then read aloud, often in Latin, to whoever was in his shop. In this store, which my friends and I used to call 'the old man's shop', I found and bought a number of old world atlases. Most of them were published between the two World Wars. I used to spend hours leafing through them, admiring their beautifully drawn maps.

Studying these maps stimulated my interest in history. I was fascinated by the way boundaries kept shifting during the first 45 years of the 20th century. Years later, I read a book, "*Between East and West*", by Anne Applebaum in which she quotes a man in the city of Brest - once in Poland, then a few years later in the USSR, and now in Belarus - as saying, "*No one around here knows if he is Belarusian, Polish, Russian...*"

It was not only the borders of Central Europe and Russia that kept moving, but also of those located further south in the Balkans. I wondered why the town of Zadar, located at the end of a peninsula of Yugoslav Dalmatia was once part of Italy although it was separated from the rest of the country by the Adriatic Sea, and why a large part of what is now western Slovenia was once Austrian before becoming part of Italy's Venezia Giulia region, and then why the town of Gorizia (now also 'Nova Gorica'), which was once Italian, is now, like Berlin used to be, a city divided by an international frontier.

One day, whilst examining one of my atlases, I saw a country, which I had not noticed before. It was Albania. I have no idea why I had not previously noticed this small country bounded by Yugoslavia, Greece, and the Adriatic Sea. My curiosity about it was aroused.

I asked Frank, my close friend and fellow book-store browser, about Albania. He had (and still does have) an encyclopaedic brain, especially where matters of geography and history were concerned. When I learnt from him that Albania was ruled by a dictatorship, which did its utmost to isolate its country's population from the outside world, my interest was fired. I decided to search high and low in order to find more information about this mysterious place and its people. What began as idle curiosity soon became an obsession.

In the 1960s, there was no internet and exceedingly little interest in Albania. So, my investigation was bound to develop slowly. My parents had a road atlas of Europe published by the Swiss company Hallwag. It included an appendix, which contained a brief guide to each of the countries of Europe shown in the maps. There were two short paragraphs about Albania. These were probably included for completeness, but I imagine that their brevity was an indication of the publisher's belief that hardly any of the users of their volume would ever find themselves driving their vehicles through Albania. Nevertheless, alongside the short text there was a tiny, grainy black and white picture of Skanderbeg Square in the heart of the capital, Tirana. The photograph showed a mosque with its single minaret standing by the square. It was the first picture of Albania that I had ever seen, and it made its capital look like truly exotic.

I had a Phillips radio in my bedroom. It was a valve radio, rather than the more modern transistor-based instruments, which were already available in the 1960s. Once it had warmed up - a slow business taking up to a minute - and had stopped emitting crackling sounds, it was able to receive broadcasts on three wavebands including short-wave. I used to enjoy twiddling its tuning knob, and listening to broadcasts transmitted from all over the world. It was a window to the world beyond the confines of the highly manicured, desirable but rather dull, Hampstead Garden Suburb, where we lived.

The author's childhood home in Hampstead Garden Suburb

One day, I tuned in on an exceptionally clear transmission, and listened with some curiosity and a great amount of surprise to a woman who was speaking perfect English with only the hint of a foreign accent. After a few minutes, she informed her audience far and wide that they were listening to the voice of Radio Tirana. I could not believe my ears. I made a mark on the tuning gauge to ensure that I would be able to find this station again. I tuned into Radio Tirana regularly, listening with astonishment and also amusement at the various commentators' beautifully articulated words - mostly rants and raves directed against the actions of the imperialists and capitalists. These were punctuated by stirring Albanian songs sung in a style that was new to me, as I had never experienced the music of the Balkans before. Incidentally, the clarity of the transmissions from Tirana was due to it being broadcast from a reputedly very powerful transmitter.

After a short while, I decided to write a letter to Radio Tirana. Somewhat tongue in cheek, I wrote to the unknown addressee (in English) that the songs, which were being broadcasted from Albania, inspired me greatly and helped to reinforce my faith in Socialism. After addressing the letter's envelope to '*Radio Tirana, Tirana, Albania*', I waited with little expectation of receiving any kind of reply. I thought that it was more likely that I would receive a communication from MI5 or MI6 than anything from Albania. However, I was wrong to have been so pessimistic. A flat parcel, wrapped in brown paper and string, arrived by post a few weeks later. It was from Albania. I unwrapped it carefully, my fingers thrilling at the thought of handling something that had arrived from the mysterious country that had begun to interest me so greatly.

The package contained a 10-inch diameter long-playing gramophone record in a garishly coloured cardboard sleeve. It was decorated with an electricity pylon; musicians in folk costumes; dancers dressed likewise; a man wearing baggy Turkish-style pantaloons; and an oil derrick. The plain, unadorned record label bore the name of the recording company:

Pllake Shqipetare ('*Shqipëria*' being the Albanian word for Albania). I played this endlessly, much to the dismay of my parents who did not appreciate its special musical properties. Even today, I can still hear the tune of "*O djell i ri*" (a song about the sun) ringing in my head.

At about the same time as I received the record, I began to stumble upon occasional bits of literature about Albania. An uncle gave me a copy of the *National Geographic* magazine that contained a few photographs of Albania. The Albanians sent me a second package, which contained a coloured magazine about life in Albania. Although it was filled with propaganda, it did contain photographs that helped me visualise the country that was beginning to intrigue me more and more.

I must have passed my 16th birthday when, during a visit to Foyle's - the enormous bookshop on Tottenham Court Road - I discovered a copy of S.E.Mann's textbook of Albanian grammar. Although it was published in 1932, the bookshop was selling this dust-covered book as new. It may have been on the shop's shelves for at least 30 years. Its price was fifteen shillings (£0.75), which was way beyond my budget when I found it. Week after week, I used to visit the shop and look at the book longingly. Eventually in 1969, an opportunity to purchase it arose. I won the 2nd prize in the Bodkin Biology Essay Competition at Highgate School for my learned discourse on the life and habits of woodlice. The first prize was awarded to Timothy, whose older brother was to become the Home Secretary under a Labour government many years later. It would be immodest if I omitted to mention that there were only two contestants in this competition!

My prize was fifteen shillings to be spent on books, one of which had to be a hardback. Mann's grammar fitted the requirements, so I thought before telling the school that it was the book I desired as my prize. I submitted my request. A few days later, the Headmaster's Secretary informed me, without displaying any sign of regret, that the school was not prepared to give me Mann's Albanian grammar as a prize, and that I needed to select something else. No reason was supplied. I was furious, but that did not help me obtain a copy of a book that is now worth many times its price in 1969.

Had I obtained the book that I yearned for, I doubt that I would have bothered to learn Albanian - a language which makes great use of the letters 'x' and 'q' (often not followed by a 'u'). Although it is a member of the great Indo-European language family, Albanian, which bears a little resemblance to Latin, sits on its own little branch of the Indo-European family tree. Today, many decades after winning that 2nd prize in the Bodkin Essay Competition, I do use my tiny vocabulary of Albanian words to put my many Albanian-speaking dental patients at ease, or simply to bring a smile to their faces.

I used to draw a great deal during my teens. For a while, I was interested in becoming an architect. I made drawings and plans of imaginary buildings, and read books about modern architecture and architects. As a result of my fascination with cartography, I also drew maps of non-existent places. In time, my curiosity about Eastern Europe, and Albania in particular, began to dominate my mind to such an extent that I decided to invent a country with the attributes of the places that I investigated and yearned to visit eventually. My creation of the land of 'Nastrovia' was a way for me to express my fascination with the region of the world that interested me so much to others.

Nastrovia, landlocked, was inserted between Poland and Hungary, and bordered to the east by the USSR. Czechoslovakia was to its west. I suppose, on reflection, Nastrovia would have had to be located where the Slovak Republic lies today. Nastrovia, although its language employed a modified Cyrillic script, was no ally of the USSR. Its only European ally was - yes, you have guessed it - Albania. The 'Nastrosocialists' governed the country with an iron fist, and had no intention of relinquishing power.

While most of my school friends were dating girls and partying in their spare time, I spent hours hunched over my desk drawing pictures of the country, its flags and emblems, its buildings, its people, and its landscape. I designed complicated visa application forms, whose questions were deliberately phrased in poor English; railway timetables written in Cyrillic; and tourist brochures for prospective visitors to Nastrovia. I began writing a textbook of the Nastrovian language, but had to give up after about 10 pages - grammar has never been one of my strongest points.

I drew maps of the country, including its capital Strektol, which had a stadium, which looked remarkably similar to the one in Nuremberg where the Nazis held their rallies in the 1930s. My finest tipped Rotring pen was used to create an incredibly detailed map of Plek, a workers' resort on the shores of Lake Gravov - an allusion to Hungary's Lake Balaton. And, as a result of my fascination with road atlases, I commenced work on an atlas of Nastrovia, whose detail even the Michelin Company would have admired. Every road and settlement in Nastrovia was marked on it, each name being written in Nastrovian Cyrillic. In keeping with the impersonal nature of some of the regimes that interested me, some places were given numbers rather than names. The style of the mapmaking was based on that of a 1950s Hungarian road atlas, which I had bought second-hand at Foyle's. I believe that I finished the first 24 of a projected 72 pages of the atlas before I gave up on it.

When I first invited the girl, who would become my wife many years later, to our house, I took her upstairs to my bedroom. I often wonder what my mother thought that we were doing whilst we were up there. She had little to worry about - or maybe a great deal. I was too busy showing Lopa my Nastrovian project to think of doing anything else.

One evening after dinner, I was sitting with my parents in the living room when my mother lowered the newspaper that she was reading, and said:

"You'll never believe this, Adam."

She handed me her paper and pointed at one of the many classified advertisements in it. It announced that there was to be a meeting of the 'Old Nastrovians'. I was astounded. I had not known when I dreamed up the name that 'Nastrovia' and its variants is the word used before downing a glass of alcohol in countries like Poland and Czechoslovakia. On another occasion, I spotted a notice announcing the meeting of the "Old Albanians". My excitement at this discovery was soon extinguished when I realised that the people who were about to meet were not real Albanians, but were rugby football players who had attended St Albans School in Hertfordshire!

Every summer until I was 18, I visited Venice and Florence with my parents. They were attracted to these cities by their love of art, its history, and the Italians. During one of those visits, I found an intriguing book in an antiquarian bookshop in Florence. It was "*Grecia*", a guidebook to Greece published, to quote its opening page exactly, in: "*Milano 1941 (XIX)*". The 'XIX' refers to the 19th year of Mussolini's reign as Italy's dictator. The book was published for his soldiers, who were marching via Albania to Greece. Its owner, Antonio Bonaldi of the 36th Battalion of Mortars, had written his name in it as well as marking its folding map with red pencil to show the route he took whilst crossing Albania. He landed in Durrës and marched towards Albania's frontier with Greece via Elbasan, Pogradec, and Korçë. According to his handwritten note he crossed into Greece on the 11th of June 1941 at Bilisht. Elsewhere in the book, there are other notes that the invading soldier added in pencil. I still get a shiver running down my spine when I consider that I am handling a book that has such an intimate association with an historical event, even if it was Mussolini's less than successful invasion of Greece.

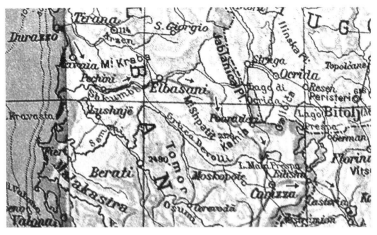

Bonaldi's route across Albania in 1941 drawn in pencil
(I have added the arrows)

Maps of Albania were almost impossible to find in London in the 1960s and 1970s. Almost nobody needed them. I used to enjoy browsing through the ground floor of Stanford's map-shop in Longacre, but never found a map of Albania there. Naturally, the maps on display were aimed at people who were most likely to buy them and then use them. The basement of the shop, which was not arranged for browsing, held a stock of detailed maps for purchasers with special requirements. It was there that I bought the shop's only copy of "*Karte von Albanien*". This detailed map (scale of 1:200,000) covered Albania in two enormous sheets and had last been revised in 1925. As the set was priced 23 shillings rather than its decimal equivalent of £1.15, I must have bought it before our currency was decimalised in early 1971. This out-of-date map remains the most detailed that I have seen of Albania to this day.

The years passed. I continued to haunt second-hand booksellers. When at last I began earning my own money after having been a student for what many may consider to have been an excessive number of years, I used to buy books from catalogues of booksellers who specialised in books about Eastern Europe. Gradually my library of books on Albania grew. I was pleased to acquire a first edition of ME Durham's book *High Albania*, which describes her trips to visit and study the Catholic tribes who inhabited the mountain wastes of northern Albania. Harry Hamm's account of his visit to the country is another one of my favourites. He was a German journalist, who visited Albania on the eve of the country's love affair with Mao's China. A chapter in a book of travel essays by James Cameron described the package trip he joined in order to visit Albania. This account whetted my appetite - I became determined to visit the country that had burrowed its way deep into my mind.

I had known for a long while that it was impossible for individuals to visit Albania as tourists, and that the only way to visit it was to join a tour group. In the 1960s and 1970s, the only British travel company offering tours to Albania was one based in Yorkshire. I had looked into what they had on offer, but was discouraged from getting involved because it seemed that their tours were designed for travellers with a particular interest in socialism rather than Albania. My politics, naïve as they were at the time, and as they are even now, did not include much sympathy with Albania's brand of socialism. I would have felt uneasy being surrounded by 'true believers' for a fortnight or so. Also, I had an aversion to travelling with groups, which has lasted to the present. So, for many years, I tried to satisfy my desire to see Albania by visiting places that were close enough for me to catch a glimpse of it.

My first ever view of Albania was from an aeroplane. I was travelling from Italy to Greece with my family when I recognised a distinctive feature of the coastline. From my vantage point 30,000 feet above the sea, I saw the Bay of Vlorë and near to it the Island of Sazan - an Albanian island on the eastern side of the Straits of Otranto, which had been part of Italy until the end of the Second World War.

My next close encounter with the country was from the sea. Sometime during the late 1960s, soon after the Greek military junta had assumed power, our family was invited to Greece as guests of a generous Greek multimillionaire. An astute reader will wonder why we accepted his offer to visit a country that was governed by a non-elected regime. My parents, who were reluctant at first, gave in when I said that as guests of our friend we would be contributing little if anything to Greece's economy. You can imagine their chagrin when they were introduced to Colonel Patakos, one of the architects of the Military Junta, and had to shake hands with him at a party arranged by our host.

Our wealthy host put us on board a luxurious yacht with 8 en-suite passenger cabins. We sailed all the way from Athens to Corfu and back. Although we did not spend long in Corfu, we did dock in Kerkyra, the island's capital. Using the captain's powerful binoculars, I peered in the direction of Albania, and believed that the faint green shore that I spied on the horizon was the southern extreme of the country, which interested me so greatly even in those days. The third and more interesting attempt to sight Albania was one which I made with my friend Richard.

My family and Richard's were staying in Greece as guests of our wealthy Greek friend. I managed to persuade Richard to accompany me on an excursion to Lake Ohrid. Sportingly, he agreed to leave the luxurious hotel at Vouliagmeni, a seaside resort near Athens, and joined me on a train, which wound slowly across the mountains of central Greece towards Thessalonika. Regularly during the eight hour trip, our compartment was visited by a man selling lukewarm pork kebabs ('*souvlaki*') on wooden sticks. They were temptingly tasty, and we could not stop eating them.

Even before we changed trains at Plati, a railway junction in northern Greece, Richard was complaining of stomach ache. Thinking that he, a less experienced traveller than I, had a weak stomach compared to mine, I continued eating these tasty toxic offerings. At nightfall, we reached the northern town of Edhessa, where we had to spend the night before continuing our journey. Prior to leaving the station, we had to have our tickets punched. Richard could not wait for the official. He rushed off into a field to relieve his troubled bowels. I was feeling well, and regarded at his behaviour with scorn.

We spent the night in Edhessa's tiny Hotel Olympia, where the beds cost only 50 pence each. They were short beds, not long enough for to stretch out fully. The next morning, Richard had recovered, but I was unable to stand up, so painful was my stomach! I was unable to eat breakfast, and felt ill watching my friend consuming a bowl of yoghurt. Another train carried us to Florina, a town in the northwest corner of Greece. I remember buying rolls of toilet paper there before boarding another train consisting of a diesel locomotive and only one carriage. This took us slowly towards Niki, a village on the Greek border. Our train drew up next to a short Yugoslav train. Nothing happened for a long while. Richard and I, the only passengers, sat waiting in the heat whilst flies crawled all over us. Eventually, a Yugoslav soldier ordered us to step from the Greek carriage into the Yugoslav one. The Yugoslav train set off, we crossed the border, and travelled to the small Macedonian town of Bitola.

The sun was setting when the bus carrying us to Ohrid set off from Bitola, and it was late at night when we pitched our tent a stone's throw away from the waterside in the campsite by the shore of Lake Ohrid, just north of the town bearing the same name.

Ohrid is one of the most beautiful towns that I have visited in the Balkans. Overlooking the lake, its narrow streets are lined by Balkan/Turkish-style dwellings with overhanging upper stories. There are Orthodox churches containing ancient frescos; mosques with picturesque minarets; a castle; and extensive ancient ruins. Small restaurants served local specialities including meats cooked on braziers over glowing charcoal. From the waterfront, the shore of Albania was visible across the lake. As I looked at the line of white marker buoys delineating the border between Yugoslavia and Albania, a thrill travelled down my spine.

Richard was content to spend his time sunning himself on the shore of the lake at our campsite and munching watermelons, but I occupied my days exploring Ohrid and making excursions to nearby places on local buses. I visited the Monastery of Sveti Naum, which sits on the border of Yugoslavia within spitting distance of Albania. I also made a trip north of the lake to the town of Debar. This small place, less than 1 ½ miles from Albania, fascinated me. Most of its inhabitants were ethnically Albanian and many of the men I saw were wearing traditional white woollen costumes with black trimmings.

Albanian men, 1909

One hot day, when I was walking back to the campsite from the town of Ohrid, I passed one of the numerous smallholdings, which lined the road, and one of the employees from the campsite greeted me. He invited me into his house. After stepping through his dung-splattered yard, which contained a donkey, a cow, and some chickens running wild, he introduced me to his family who were squatting on pillows placed around the walls of a small living room. He asked me whether I wanted some milk. As it was a swelteringly warm day and I was thirsty, I said yes, or, more likely, '*da*'. Instead of a condensation-coated chilled glass of chilled milk that I was hoping to receive, I was handed a glass warm slightly off-white liquid. As I brought it close to my mouth, its smell made me nauseous. I took a small sip, hoping that I would not abuse my hosts' hospitality by vomiting. I did not. After a short while, I shook hands with the hospitable head of the household, and smiled at everyone else before continuing on my way, hoping that my inability to finish the drink had not offended them.

I revisited the Yugoslav shore of Lake Ohrid several times before I went to Albania. Once, I visited the place with a group of friends from Belgrade. We flew into Ohrid's small airport, which was located close to Struga, a village at the north end of the lake. The approach to this place was spectacular because to reach the runway the plane had to swoop downwards towards the lake beneath us. It seemed as if we were about to land on the water. We visited the monastery of Sveti Naum which is located at the southern end of the lake. It is famous for its fine frescos, but that was not its main attraction for me. What really intrigued me was that it was located only a few yards from the Albanian border. We wandered around the monastery's gardens, and approached the border so closely that the Albanian soldiers guarding it began to look quite worried.

My third visit to Ohrid was brief. I was travelling to Platamon in northern Greece by road with Robert Harkness, my PhD supervisor and Margaret, his wife. I persuaded them to deviate from their usual route, which took them through Skopje, and to go via Ohrid instead. After stopping briefly at Tetovo, where we viewed the *tekke* in which dervishes used to whirl under its beautifully decorated ceiling, we arrived at Lake Ohrid.

The Harknesses, who travelled with a caravan towed by an ancient long-wheelbase Land Rover, were averse to camping in organised camp-sites. Reluctantly, they became reconciled to spending the night at Ohrid's camp-site, as they were unable to find anywhere safe enough to camp 'wild'. It was the same site where Richard and I had camped many years before. Imagine my surprise when an elderly employee came up to me and greeted me like a long lost friend. It was the same man who had been so hospitable when I first visited Ohrid. This time, he did not offer me milk.

Whilst I was a doctoral student at University College London during the early 1970s, I made great use of its excellent library facilities, both for my scientific research and also to pursue other interests. I found a copy of Edward Lear's account of his trip to Greece and Albania. In my student days, it was possible to borrow books as valuable as this, and to take them home. Today, I imagine that Lear's book would not be available on open shelves, and certainly not borrowable. From what I remember, Lear was not particularly enamoured of Albania. However, he produced some beautiful illustrations despite the local children throwing stones at him whilst he tried to sketch, and the generally uncomfortable times that he spent travelling around the country. For my 21st birthday, the Harknesses, familiar with my great interest in the Balkans, gave me an old lithograph based on one of Lear's paintings. Its subject was not of Albania, but it was drawn during the trip that Lear made to Albania. It depicts some of the monasteries at Meteora in central Greece, which I had visited with Robert and Margaret.

On another holiday, I left Platamon, where I had been camping by the sea with Robert and Margaret, and took a train to the city of Skopje in Yugoslav Macedonia. I did not plan to linger there because I was under the impression that it had been completely rebuilt after the devastating earthquake that hit it in 1963. When I arrived, I had a few hours to look around, and was pleasantly surprised to discover how much of the old city had remained intact.

I was the only foreigner boarding a long-distance bus at Skopje. It was bound for Prizren. My fellow passengers stared at me, and

I looked at them, surprised by their generally unhealthy appearances. Most of them looked thin and their complexions were mostly pasty. After a four hour journey we arrived at our destination. It was in the heart of what was then called the '*Autonomous Province of Kosovo & Methohija*', a troubled region, historically of great importance to the Serbs, where the majority of the inhabitants were ethnically Albanian.

When I disembarked at the bus station with my rucksack on my back, I was immediately surrounded by people, mostly young men. Everyone wanted to know my name, rather than my nationality or where I had come from. When I said it was 'Adam', they then asked me whether I was a Moslem. The answer did not seem to matter to them; they were just pleased to meet a stranger. When they had worked out that I needed somewhere to stay, they led me to a campsite, where I was able to rent a most reasonably priced holiday chalet - I had no tent. These people were all as Albanian as those who would many years later wave to me cautiously in Gjirokastër (in Albania), but as their lives were not dominated by the Sigurimi (the Albanian secret police), they were able to be open and friendly to a stranger like me.

Apart from the presence of Albanians, the beautiful old Orthodox churches, the mosques and the generally pleasant feel of the well-watered place, there was yet another thing that attracted me to Prizren. All of the street name signs were trilingual: Serbian, Albanian, and Turkish. Some of the town's population were Turkish, no doubt left behind when the Ottoman Empire dissolved. I noticed at the bus-station that there was even a regular bus service between Prizren and Istanbul.

After spending a couple of days in Prizren, I took a bus to Peć ('*Pejë*' in Albanian), where I had hoped to visit the celebrated ancient Serbian Orthodox Patriarchate in its outskirts. I was unable to do this because a bout of diarrhoea kept me confined to within easy walking distance of my hotel room, which had its own decent enough toilet. Whilst exploring the town, I walked past a hospital. It was surrounded by people, who were loading baskets, which were then hauled on ropes to its upper storeys by patients who were leaning out of open windows. I never discovered what these baskets contained, but it was most likely to have been food. The next day, my innards having recovered, I left Peć and Kosovo.

In the 1970s, when I made that visit, the Autonomous Region was quiet, not at all crowded. Many years later, in 1991, when I made my last visit to the former Yugoslavia, I revisited Kosovo with my Serbian friend Raša. We were staying at a monastery in Macedonia, and drove from there to Priština, the capital of Kosovo. We drove over a pass between Macedonia and the Autonomous Region. As soon as we entered the latter, the landscape changed dramatically. During the decade or so since I had last visited the area, the countryside had become heavily built-up. Even outside the towns and villages, there were swarms of recently built dwellings. There were people everywhere. Driving was made difficult because of the crowds of pedestrians and animals on the roads. In the villages and towns it was necessary to drive patiently and slowly without sounding the horn - Raša advised against using the horn to avoid annoying the locals, who might have got angry if we, who were obviously not local people, had shown signs of impatience. He felt that it was wise to wait for people to get out of the way when they felt like doing so. I had never driven in such conditions before, and was not to do so again until I visited India a few years later.

Before Raša and I set off from Belgrade to make that trip in May 1991, Raša advised me to book the hire car, in which we were going to travel, from Avis rather than Hertz because in that way we would be in a car bearing Slovenian rather than Serbian registration plates. A few months before we travelled to Kosovo, a number of Serbs living in Kosovo had been killed by their Albanian neighbours. Raša believed that we would be safer in a car that appeared to come from Slovenia. He was extremely fluent in English, and decided that he would be safer if he only spoke English whilst in Kosovo, which he sportingly agreed to visit with me as my 39th birthday treat. In addition to visiting Priština and some beautiful Orthodox monasteries in the region, we stopped briefly in Gnjilane, a town where many Serbs had been killed a few months earlier. When I pointed out a kebab shop, whose sign used a modification of the McDonald's logo, he turned to me and said:

"Anything's possible here in Kosovo. This is the Wild West."

Our visit to Kosovo was part of a ten day tour we were making around the Federal Republic of Serbia. At each place we stopped, Raša spoke to many local people, especially the learned Serbian Orthodox priests in the monasteries, which we visited. Gradually, as we drove around Serbia, Raša told me what these people had told him. He was able to make what turned out to be an accurate prediction of the painful break-up of Yugoslavia, which began soon after I left. At the end of the trip, he came to see me off at Belgrade's airport. As I waved to him before entering the departure lounge, I looked at him and had a strange presentiment. I felt that he knew that we were seeing each other for the last time. He died a few years later, soon after both the Bosnian and Kosovo Wars were over.

Returning to the trip, which I made in the 1970s, I travelled from Peć to Titograd by bus. I chose to take the route that went via the wild and difficult Ĉakor Pass that traverses the mountain range shared by northern Albania and Montenegro, where I was heading. We reached the highest point on the pass after driving around a seemingly endless series of tight hairpin bends, and stopped there to give the driver a break. Whilst I was wandering around the treeless, grassy summit, admiring the views into the valley into which we would be descending, a grubby little boy approached me. He said something to me in a language, which I did not recognise as being Serbo-Croat. It was probably

Albanian. Somehow, he made it clear to me that he wanted foreign coins. I thought that he was either a beggar, or more likely, just a curious youngster pleased to have chanced upon a foreigner. I gave him a few British coins, and then he rummaged around in his pocket. After a moment, he handed me a few Yugoslav Dinar coins, and left. He was no beggar, after all, but simply a young fellow with a well-developed sense of fairness. After leaving the Ĉakor, we wound through the mountains to Andrijevica, a small Montenegrin town, which was enshrouded in rain and mist. Then, we descended gradually via a series of deep wooded canyons towards Titograd. All I saw of the town on that occasion was its bus station. Little did I realise then that a few years later I would be spending a night there at the beginning of a great adventure.

"Sketching on the bridge and on the west side of the town occupied me for two or three hours. The women of Berat are all veiled. They wear a close-fitting, dark blue cloth vest, or pelisse, not at all unbecoming; and their very thin muslin 'face-cover' is so well and cleverly adjusted, particularly by the younger and pretty part of the female population - and these are numerous - that the outline of the features can easily be distinguished."

[Edward Lear, 1851]

Philip Ward

By the beginning of the 1980s, I had flown over Albania, seen its coast from Greece, approached it to within a few feet of its border at Sveti Naum, met Albanian people in Kosovo, and 'circumnavigated' its land borders. Now, all that remained was to visit the place, and the opportunity soon presented itself.

Late in 1982, Philip Ward published his *"Albania: A Travel Guide"*. I bought a copy in 1983. This well-illustrated publication, which is both a guidebook and a travelogue, was the key to realising my long-held desire to visit Albania. Apart from being one of the best guidebooks to Albania that has been published during the past 30 years, it provides a description of the tour that the author had just made in Albania. Ward travelled around the country as a member of a group tour organised by Regents Holidays, a Bristol based company. From what he wrote, it was clear that he had visited a wide range of places in the country, and that what the company was offering was attractive enough to overcome my prejudices against package holidays. I sent for, and then filled in an application form, which I returned with my cheque to Regents Holidays.

I spent the weekend before my departure with my friends Robert and Margaret Harkness at Rough Hey, their enormous, now demolished, Victorian pile near Stoke Poges in Buckinghamshire. They had a tennis court in their large garden, and used to ask me to be the fourth player in doubles matches. I was a hopeless player, but I could serve reasonably accurately and return a few shots (occasionally). That weekend, whilst on the court, I felt something give way suddenly in one of my knees. As it was not painful, I did not mention it. However, when we walked back to the house to take afternoon tea, I noticed that my leg was not moving normally. It seemed to flick out sideways while I walked. I decided to keep quiet about this problem, and hoped that nobody would notice it. The last thing I wanted was to have to cancel my forthcoming trip to Albania. I felt that providing I made it onto the aeroplane, all would be well. If my leg's condition worsened, there would have been some kind of medical care available in Albania. As it happened, it righted itself after a few days.

So, in April 1984, I joined my fellow travellers at Heathrow Airport. To my great relief they only included a few true believers of the socialist variety. We were ready to embark on a Regents Holidays trip to visit to the country, which had been on my mind for more than one and a half decades.

Gjirokastër, 1927

"All the same, the Minister went on, the men should be observed with the greatest discretion so as not to alert them in the slightest, and generally speaking, the authorities of N- were to behave in such a manner to make the foreigners feel quite at home."

[Ismail Kadare, 1996]

IN ENVER'S ALBANIA

Reminiscences of a visit to Albania in 1984

The wheels of the Jugoslovenski Aerotransport ('JAT') jet thudded firmly onto the skid-stained concrete runway at Belgrade's Surčin Airport. Noisily, its elevated ailerons decelerated the aircraft. And, as they did so, the passengers around me applauded, some of them also crossing themselves in gratitude for a safe landing. We disembarked and walked to the bus that was waiting to carry us to the terminal building, where we completed immigration formalities and reclaimed our baggage. When this was done, we discovered that we had to wait for at least four hours before we were to be called for our next flight.

I was a regular visitor to Yugoslavia, and just happened to have a few Dinar coins in my pocket. Knowing that I had some time on my hands, I decided to find a public telephone, and ring some of my friends who lived in Belgrade. I managed to get through to Lilja. We agreed to meet for a quick coffee at the city air terminal, which was located in the city at one end of Bulevar Revolucije, about twelve miles from the airport. Less than half an hour after leaving the airport, I found her waiting for me at a table in a café next to the stop where I disembarked from the airport bus. We drunk coffee together, gossiped a little, and then I boarded a bus that took me back to Surčin.

I rejoined the other members of the group with whom I was travelling. Although we had barely got to know each other, our English tour leader, Julian, was surprised and possibly concerned by my separation from the rest of the group, which had remained with him, waiting at the airport. In hindsight, my brief excursion into central Belgrade was a bit rash. Had I been delayed in town for any reason, I would have missed the next flight and also, more importantly, the chance of visiting Albania.

We filed through the departure gate in order to board our domestic flight on a JAT jet bound for Titograd (currently known as 'Podgorica', its pre-WW2 name). Before we were allowed to board our aeroplane, we had to enter a hangar where all of our baggage was laid out on the floor. We had to point out our pieces of luggage to the airline staff. Only items of baggage that had been identified were allowed to be stowed in the aircraft. This was to ensure that each thing in the hold belonged to someone who had actually boarded the aeroplane. The theory was that people, who had boarded, were unlikely to want to travel on a 'plane that was likely to explode midflight. Many years later, I encountered this same anti-terrorism precaution when boarding flights in India.

Our 'plane touched down in Titograd in the late afternoon, and we were taken in a coach to a modern hotel, the 'Podgorica', which still serves visitors today. It was a grey concrete structure, straggling along the side of a shallow ravine at the bottom of which the River Moraca flowed. In order to save money I had not paid the supplementary fee for a single room. So, after entering the Podgorica's lobby, I waited with some trepidation to see with whom I would be sharing a room for the next fortnight. My room mate Jerry was a teacher in an adult education centre. He was married, but had decided to visit Albania whilst his Romanian wife was visiting his in-laws in Romania with his son. As he found that these family visits were somewhat tedious, he tended to avoid them and used the time to make trips to places that interested him, but were unlikely to be enjoyable for the rest of his family. He and I shared an interest in Albania. Our meeting in Titograd marked the beginning of a long-lasting friendship.

After eating breakfast at the Podgorica the next morning, we boarded a Yugoslav coach with a local guide, an elderly gentleman dressed in a formal dark suit. He informed us that he would take us on a brief sight-seeing tour of Titograd. We drove slowly along a long, wide street.

"Here is one post office," our guide explained as we passed a building on our left.

And then, a few moments later:

"Here is one theatre."

And then:

"Here is one park."

Followed by:

"Here is one monument to our brave partisans."

Having seen those sights, our bus made a u-turn, and we began returning the way we had come.

"Here is one monument to our brave partisans," the elderly gentleman explained enthusiastically.

"Here is one park," he informed us an instant later.

"Here is one theatre," we learnt.

"Here is one post office," our guide explained as we passed a building on our right.

And, with that, our tour of Titograd was successfully completed. Our venerable dragoman disembarked, and then we made our way across a plain towards Lake Skadar ('Shkodër', in Albanian), a body of water close to the Adriatic coast, and shared between Yugoslavia and Albania.

We arrived at the Yugoslav frontier post on the eastern shore of the lake. Acres of reeds hid its distant watery horizon from our view. Our bus drew up next to the few buildings that housed the Yugoslav customs and immigration offices. We disembarked from our coach and collected all of our baggage, which in my case was only a rucksack. I don't remember there having been any dealings with the Yugoslav officials before we were instructed to walk with our belongings along the road leading towards Albania. It was devoid of traffic: there were no other vehicles or people in sight. Apart from us and a few birds high above us, no one was entering or leaving Albania.

About 100 yards south of where our coach had disgorged us, we encountered an Albanian soldier. He was standing statue-like in the middle of the road. He was a remarkable, proud-looking man, whose uniform did little to disguise his muscular physique. His hands clasped a rifle held diagonally across his chest. This monument-like character appeared not to notice us, or, at least, he showed no sign that he did. Julian, our Regents Holidays tour guide, stood near him and collected our passports as we filed passed him. As we surrendered our documents, he explained to each of us that we were being admitted into Albania on a 'group visa'. The implications of this were to become evident later on when we were well ensconced in our tour of Enver Hoxha's Balkan paradise.

We were ushered politely into the Albanian customs house. There was a slogan in English on the wall immediately opposite the entrance, which proclaimed: *"Even if we have to go without bread, we Albanians do not violate principles. We will not betray Marxism - Leninism."* It was written in capitals using faded red letters that looked like those used to advertise films on the canopies above the entrances to cinemas. All of the letters were firmly attached to the wall except one. This was detachable as it had been glued onto a removable hatch cover, which must have provided access to services - plumbing or wiring - hidden within the wall. The room was filled with comfortable armchairs, each one provided with a white lacy anti-macassar. We sat in these, and then filled in the detailed custom declaration form that needed to know whether we would be importing, amongst a variety of other items, any *'magnétophones'* or *'frigidaires'*. As I filled in my form, I wondered who, apart from diplomats, visited the country laden with goods such as these. Two by two, we were summoned up to be interviewed by the customs officers standing behind tables.

In each of the bedrooms of the Hotel Podgorica at Titograd, there were some illustrated leaflets, which were designed to encourage tourism in Montenegro. I ignored these because I had visited Montenegro before. Also, apart from being of little interest they were poorly illustrated. However, many in our group had taken them as souvenirs. It was these that customs officers were seeking. The reason for their quest was that there was a very grainy, small colour photograph of bathers on a nudist beach in one of them. If this picture was examined carefully, and one knew in advance that its subject was a nudist beach, it would have been almost possible to believe that the people in the picture were devoid of clothing. It was this poorly reproduced image that the Albanian officials were seeking in their attempt to prevent pornographic material from entering the Motherland. Whenever they found one, they confiscated it, but not before labelling it with its owner's name.

Eventually, the customs examination was completed. We boarded the Albanian coach, a vehicle made in Italy, in which we were going to be transported during the next 14 days. Once on board, we were introduced to our three Albanian crew members. They were going to accompany us throughout our trip. The driver, whose name I never learnt, was the oldest and most senior. He was a member of the Albanian Communist Party we discovered later. He was a pleasant fellow, who was able to converse in a remarkable number of languages. Aferdita was the daughter of one of Albania's few international judges, and was thus a representative of the country's socialist 'aristocracy', its equivalent to the Soviet *Nomenklatura.* She spoke excellent English, and had a sunny personality. Eduart, the third member of the Albanian team, was quite different. During the fortnight that we spent in his company, it became evident that he might well have been an ambitious and keen young member of the *Sigurimi*, the country's much-feared secret police, who were only identifiable, so I was told, by the characteristic belt buckles, which they wore.

We drove away from the border post, passing numerous seemingly randomly placed hemispherical concrete bunkers with horizontal slits piercing them. These miniature bunkers, large enough to accommodate two or three adults, looked like giant pimples and were liberally peppered throughout the whole country. They were part of Albania's defence against foreign invaders. After having been occupied by the Turks, Italians, and the Germans, Enver Hoxha's regime was determined that their country should never again be overrun by foreign armies. The enemies of Hoxha's establishment were many. They included the capitalist countries and the 'wicked imperialists', which meant most of the so-called Western nations. However, there were also countries with communist regimes, which had once been regarded as friendly by Albania, although for brief periods, that were now regarded as being hostile. Amongst these was the Soviet Union (and its allies), which had abandoned Hoxha's hero Stalin and also Stalinism; Yugoslavia, which was happy to be courted by the West; and the Peoples Republic of China, a former ally who was also beginning to flirt with its former capitalist foes - President Nixon had visited the country in 1972.

About a kilometre into Albania, we drove through a gap in a high wire fence, which looked as if it might well have been electrified. Its wire strands were connected to white porcelain insulators, such as are found on power lines. As few outsiders ever wandered into the country except by accident, this barrier was physical evidence of the regime's determination to prevent its subjects from straying out of it and into the wicked, hostile world outside the Marxist-Leninist paradise, which Hoxha and his associates had been creating since 1945.

There was an elderly lady on our tour. She was an octogenarian. She told some of us at Heathrow Airport that she wanted to visit Albania because she had heard that because it contained few cars and trucks it was a tranquil, quiet place. One hot day when we were out in the country, looking at some sight, which I do not recall, I walked past one of the ubiquitous bunkers. Suddenly this elderly lady emerged from within it, and called me aside.

"You know, dear," she said conspiratorially, and pointing at our coach driver. "He's keeping an eye on everybody."

She was right. We were regarded as representatives of the wicked imperialist west, and as such were potential enemies. It is not surprising that we were closely observed by our Albanian hosts throughout our visit to Enver Hoxha's workers' paradise.

Less numerous than the bunkers, but, nevertheless, not in short supply, were wedge-shaped concrete structures, which projected from the sides of roads. They were triangular (right-angled) in elevation and fronted by doors locked with padlocks. We speculated that these objects enclosed staircases that led to underground stores or shelters, which were, like the hemispherical bunkers, part of the country's self-defence system. No one ever told us what they really were, but this hypothesis seemed reasonable given the country's concerns about being overrun by foreign invaders.

Just before lunch on our first day in Albania, we drove into the city of Shkodër, which is located at the southern end of the lake with the same name. We arrived at a shabby looking hotel in the centre of town. A hemispherical bunker that bulged up from the pavement near the entrance was visible from inside the lobby, where we were waiting to be allocated rooms. I listened to one member of our party talking with the hotel's receptionist, offering to pay a supplement in order to have a single room. It was Sam, who ran a number of stalls selling jewellery on London's pavements. He said he needed a room of his own because he was an insomniac, and was concerned about disturbing his roommate's sleep. Every day during our trip, Sam made sure that his large thermos flask was filled with numerous cups of Turkish coffee. He drank this throughout the day. The resulting enormous intake of caffeine might well have been the cause of his inability to sleep at night. One of our group, a young female doctor, told me that she did not believe, despite what Sam claimed, that he did not get at least a little sleep at night. I was insufficiently knowledgeable to discuss this with her. I believe that was the only contact that I made with her during our tour. She said little to anyone.

Shkodër & its castle, 1914

Our 2nd floor bedroom window in Shkodër looked out along a wide street that stretched away towards the horizon. There was not a car, bus, or truck in sight. As far as the eye could see there were cyclists and pedestrians making their way along the highway. The scene reminded me of photographs taken in the People's Republic of China and also of the paintings of Malcolm Lowry. There was little background noise even though we were in the heart of a city. The old lady, who had come to experience the lack of traffic noise, was not going to be disappointed!

We were served lunch in the hotel's dining room. As in all the hotels, in which we stayed in Albania, our group's table was hidden from the eyes of the rest of the diners by a screen of curtains. From this first day onwards, it was clear that the controllers of the regime wanted to prevent us from making any contact with Albanians except those few, who had been specially allowed to do so. After lunch, the Australian, who was travelling with us (he was an official in his country's postal service), called me aside, looking shocked. He told me that when he was in the hotel's lift, an Albanian couple began to strike up a conversation with him, but stopped abruptly mid-sentence. It was, he felt, as if they were keen to speak to an outsider, but became scared of the consequences of being caught doing so. Maybe, they had been worried, not without reason, that the lift might have been fitted with a hidden microphone. Anything was possible in this mysterious world so well described by the Albanian novelist Ismail Kadare, some of whose novels I read long after my visit to his native land (from which he fled to live in exile in France).

After an unexceptional lunch, I roamed around the streets of Shkodër. I came across a small public garden, which was dominated by a chunky statue of Joseph Stalin. Even 30 years after his death, Albania continued to honour him. It was the only country in Europe still revering that illustrious Georgian. There was even a town, Qyteti Stalin (now known by its pre-Communist name as 'Kuçovë'), named in his memory, but we did not visit it. I am pleased that I saw this statue, because although I did see many other statues on our trip they were mostly depictions of Enver Hoxha.

I discovered a bookshop near to Stalin's monument, and being addicted to such establishments, I entered. I was surprised to find an Albanian textbook of dentistry prominently displayed there. Though crudely illustrated with line-drawings, I could make out that it was quite up-to-date. To the evident surprise of the shop's staff, I purchased it and another dental book. I still treasure these two unusual souvenirs from Shkodër.

After leaving the bookshop, I joined a small group of my tour companions, who were also wandering about. We came across a deserted street lined with well-preserved traditional Balkan buildings, a kind of heritage zone for tourists. Some of the buildings contained shops displaying a variety of handicrafts, but all of them were closed. Nearby, we stumbled across the Museum of Atheism, a place, which I had read about and that I was most curious to visit. Under the dictatorship of Enver Hoxha, religion was officially banned in Albania, and, according to our guides, it no was longer practised, but we were to discover later that this was not quite the case. Sadly, the museum was closed, and looked as if it had not been opened for a long time. A policeman, dressed in a grubby ill-fitting uniform, was standing in front of its main entrance. He made a gesture that we easily understood to mean that he was troubled by our presence.

Back at the hotel, Jerry, my room-mate, was in trouble already. A keen walker, he had decided to stretch his legs by taking a long stroll to the Rozafat Castle, which was on the top of a hill a little way outside the town. Julian, our Regent's Holiday guide, who was always keen to ingratiate himself to our Albanian hosts, told him that it had been foolish to stray so far from the rest of our group without first getting permission. Not only was individual exploration discouraged, but also, he informed Jerry, his safety could not be guaranteed because he did not have an individual visa. A traveller, who was on a group visa as we were, risked trouble from the Albanian authorities if he or she separated from the group. He had been warned! Moreover, he was told, his effort was wasted as we were on the point of visiting the castle in our coach. We did that while the light was failing before dinner.

We boarded our coach the next morning, and drove out of Shkodër to visit the multi-arched, ancient Turkish bridge at Mesi. Having admired that briefly, we returned to the centre of Shkodër, and followed another road that radiated from its centre. We reached a factory on its outskirts. We were told that it manufactured copper wire. After waiting for a heavy iron gate on rollers to be opened, we drove inside the compound. I was looking forward to visiting this establishment - I had never before visited a wire-making, or any other kind of, factory apart from Watney's brewery at Mortlake. However, before we had all disembarked, the heavens opened, and soon there were several inches of water on the poorly drained ground. We were told to get back into the bus and that our factory visit was to be aborted. It took a while to leave the compound because the electrically operated sliding main gate had become jammed in its closed position by the rain waters.

The bridge at Mesi, 1914

The centre of Shkodër, through which we had to return, was flooded. People were splashing through the inundation, some with umbrellas, many without. I was not to see such a scene again for more than 10 years, when I began visiting India, sometimes during the Monsoon season.

Some years after my return from Albania, I purchased a copy of "*Albania: the Foundling State of Europe*" by Wadham Peacock, who was private secretary to the British Consul General in Shkodër. It was published in 1914 - one year after Albania became an independent nation. Peacock recorded that in his day Shkodër was subject to flash floods frequently. So, what we experienced in 1984 was nothing new.

Our coach headed out of Shkodër along the main road leading southwards. Once we were out of town, Aferdita delivered the first of her brief daily lectures. Everyday, she treated us to a discourse on one of a variety of different aspects of life in Albania. The one that I can recall best was on the subject of medicine. She informed us, whilst we were travelling towards Sarandë some days well into our tour, that since the advent of the communists not only had malaria been eradicated, but also tuberculosis and syphilis. After extolling the virtues of her country's medical facilities, she offered to answer any questions that had arisen in our minds as a result of her lecture. No one said anything. Then, Julian, knowing already that the young lady doctor travelling with us was a reticent person, asked me, the dentist on board, to pose a question. I asked whether antibiotics were readily available in Albania. My reason for asking this was that I believed that the country, which was clearly trying to be totally self-reliant, would have been reluctant to import costly pharmaceuticals. Aferdita replied indignantly:

"Why, of course they are."

And then, spreading her hands wide apart, she exclaimed:

"When we reach the next town, I will get you a packet of antibiotics this large."

Sadly, she never fulfilled this unusually generous offer.

During another lecture that she gave, a woman with an American accent - she was an American-born British Subject travelling on a British passport (the Albanians did not permit US citizens to enter their country) - asked a question about freedom of speech. This caused Aferdita to become embarrassed, and the potentially awkward situation was only resolved when our guide Julian, a toadying lackey of the Hoxha regime, admonished the questioner for tactlessly abusing the hospitality of the Albanian people.

I believe that the lectures that we were given on the coach were not simply informative. They were supposed to teach us about the advanced nature of Albanian society. I think that the Albanians did not regard us as being simple tourists, but rather as potential messengers. We were being shown the country with a view, so our hosts hoped, to providing us with information that we could use to broadcast to the world how well Albania was progressing along the isolationist path it had chosen to take. Given the high average intelligence of those in our group, this plan to influence us with simplistic propaganda was bound to backfire.

Julian told us that he had visited Albania about 20 times. However, he appeared to have little or, more likely, no knowledge of the Albanian language. When questioned about things and places, which we were visiting, he was rarely able to answer. For him, the attraction of Albania was its communist regime, of which he was a keen supporter. I did not like him. On one occasion when I had returned from a bookshop somewhere that we had stopped, I left my bag on my seat for a few minutes. When I returned to it I saw him drawing away from it suddenly, looking rather embarrassed. I am sure that he had been rummaging through it to see what I had bought. I had the impression that he was keen to make sure that I had not found a book, which he had not seen before and that he would have liked to possess.

We stopped briefly in Lezhë, the first sizeable town south of Shkodër. Low, plain buildings made with undressed brickwork lined the main road that straggled along the length of the place. People milled around the dusty streets unhurriedly. We had stopped next to a public library. I peered inside it and saw a small room well-stocked with shelves filled with books in plain bindings. The people inside looked at me as if I had come from outer space.

A short distance away from Lezhë, we left the main road and entered a wooded reservation. We stopped outside a building, which we were told was once Mussolini's hunting lodge. In fact, it was the lodge designed by his son-in-law, Italy's former

Foreign Minister, Count Ciano. The Italians had had a very dominating influence on Albania during the 1930s. They invaded it at the end of that decade. As hunting lodges go, I cannot recall it being particularly exceptional. However, as we were walking away from it across the spongy soil through the pleasantly wooded grounds, a memorable incident occurred. One member of our group, a middle-aged lady who never made much impression on me, suddenly felt unwell. Almost immediately, two medical personnel dressed in white coats, appeared from out of the blue, and escorted her back to the lodge, where they did something to help her. I have no idea whether these medics just happened to be present by chance, or whether the authorities had arranged for our group to be shadowed by a medical team just in case an incident like this should occur. As there were no further medical emergencies during our trip, except when the young couple, who were, like Julian, Marxist-Leninist sympathisers, got food poisoning, I was unable to ascertain whether we were being trailed by a medical team all of the time. It would not have surprised me if we had been.

Given that the highway, on which we were travelling from Lezhë, was the main road between the capital Tirana and one of the country's few border crossings, there was remarkably little motorised traffic on it. There were plenty of pedestrians and cyclists, a few buses and trucks, and no saloon (or estate) cars. No one in Albania owned cars - they were only used for official purposes, or, as we were to discover later, as taxis.

Every now and then we met or passed a type of vehicle the likes of which I have never seen anywhere else during my travels. It was a horse-drawn lorry. Imagine a motorised truck with its engine compartment sliced off neatly below the driver's windscreen. What remains is a flat-fronted vehicle. Two slots cut below the part of the windscreen in front of the driver's seat allow the driver to hold the reigns of the horses that provide the truck's motive power. We encountered many of these vehicles on the roads in the country and towns during our visit to Albania.

We reached Tirana, where we were assigned rooms in the then almost new Tirana Hotel. It was located in the city's centre, and was one of the city's tallest buildings, being more than 12 stories high. The view from our bedroom was wonderful. We looked down on Skanderbeg Square, which, despite being in the heart of the country's largest city, was almost devoid of motor traffic. In addition to the infrequent appearances of often overcrowded public buses, the occasional Peugeot saloon car and Volvo estate car (the hardy, brick-shaped 240 series) would zip around the square. These foreign-built cars, and the even rarer Mercedes Benz, were used for government business. None of them were privately owned. During one of our many stays in the city, some of group claimed to have glimpsed Enver Hoxha passing by in a Mercedes, but if Lloyd Jones novel "*Biografi*" has any truth in it, they may have only seen an Enver Hoxha lookalike!

The buildings around the square were interesting. One side there stood a grand well-preserved mosque with a single minaret. A few men were sitting under its three-arched verandah. This was the building, which many years before I had seen illustrated in Hallwag's *Europa Atlas*. The 'square' was five sided. Three of the sides formed an elongated rectangle and at the end furthest from the hotel, the square narrowed into a funnel from which a long wide boulevard stretched towards the city's university. The two short sides of this funnel were lined by two identical imposing buildings, which were built in a style reminiscent of Italian Fascist architecture. Indeed, they were most probably built during that era. They were not far from the Hotel Dajti, which was also built in that style and to which I will return later. The Palace of Culture with its colonnaded facade, built, I believe, by the Russians (or, it might have been the Chinese) during their brief flirtation with Albania, stood beside the square nearer the hotel.

Everyone on our trip was surprised that we had been put up in Tirana so soon on our trip. According to the itinerary, which we had been sent prior to leaving England, we should not have been there on our second night in Albania. The itinerary provided by Regents Holidays proved to be completely inaccurate. From day to day, we had no idea where we would be staying next. I suspect that the reason for this was that Albturist, the country's state travel organisation, had limited accommodation available for foreign tourists, and since there was more than one foreign group travelling around at the same time as ours, they had to move us to wherever there was sufficient accommodation available. Maybe, I am just being paranoid, but there may have been other more subtle reasons for keeping us in the dark about our movements.

The mosque in Tirana, 1927

During this, our first, stay in Tirana, some of us accepted an invitation to attend a concert held in the Palace of Culture. As guests of honour we were directed to sit on the armchairs in the front two rows of the auditorium. The rest of the audience sat on less comfortable seats behind us. We understood that we were about to hear a recital of Schubert lieder. From the moment that the pianist began thumping the keys of her instrument, I knew that this recital would be quite unlike any other that I had attended before. She attacked her pianoforte vigorously enough to awaken the dead. And when the singers began performing the songs as if they were stirring hymns of praise to Enver Hoxha, Schubert must have turned in his grave. Their performances of his songs sounded remarkably like the folk-songs that I used enjoy hearing on the gramophone record that Radio Tirana had sent me many years before. The unusual rendering of Schubert's songs may have been a reflection of the performers' lack of exposure of to competent recordings and broadcasts of western classical music. However, this concert demonstrated that although Albania was isolated in many ways, there was at least some recognition of the cultural universe beyond the electric fences that surrounded it. Taking a paranoid view of this concert, I wonder whether it been specially arranged so that we should leave Albania thinking that it was really in touch with world culture, when it really was not.

Next day, or it may have been the day after, we left Tirana and began driving southwards towards our next destination, the historic city of Gjirokastër. The Albanian countryside was much greener and lusher than in much of Greece and southern Yugoslavia. Every available patch of land was utilised for cultivation. As we drove along mountain roads we passed intricate terracing, which allowed maximum use of the sloping land for growing crops. And, wherever one looked, as far as the eye could see, the landscape, be it flat or otherwise, was peppered with small hemispherical concrete bunkers. Even within towns, these defensive domes erupted from the ground like some pernicious skin disease.

We reached Gjirokastër just before lunch. Our hotel, located near a small market a short distance from the historic centre of the city, had a rustic feel about it and looked as if it had been designed by someone with a preference for traditional architecture. Our bedroom resembled many that I had stayed in when travelling off the beaten track in the Balkans, but it had one feature that made it unique. It contained two pairs of rubber flip-flops. These were presumably for the use of guests to prevent their feet from being chilled where the threadbare carpets failed to cover the room's stone flooring. This was a nice idea, which is found elsewhere in the world only in some luxury hotels, where soft towelling slippers, rather than flip-flops, are provided to guests.

Our first meal in Gjirokastër was lunch. We were served meat, vegetables, salad, and pommes-frites, as we had been for all the previous meals. The fare was what used to be called 'continental' in British restaurants prior to the 1960s. It was competently cooked, but unexciting. That lunchtime, as we sat eating in our dining area specially segregated from the local diners, we told Aferdita and Eduart that we were keen to try Albanian cuisine. To their credit, and my surprise, they listened to us. For the rest of the trip, we were served Albanian dishes, most of which differed little from Turkish-influenced fare served elsewhere in the Balkans. *Tarator*, a cold yoghurt soup containing shreds of cucumber and a lot of garlic was one of my favourite dishes in Albania. It resembled a liquid version of the Greek dip tzatziki. Mineral water was always served. Some of the unopened bottles placed in front of us had tiny green flakes floating about gently within the water. We all drank this without ill-effect. In fact the only people to have complained about food-poisoning were the two young socialist sycophants, whom I have already mentioned.

Alcohol was also available at meals for a small supplementary payment. Maynard, one of the more entertaining members of our party, was fascinated by Albanian wine. At every meal, he ordered a bottle and then made a great show of sniffing its bouquet as if it were a fine vintage from a famous French chateau. Sadly, the wines we were served only proved the importance of the absence of French savoir-faire in the Albanian wine industry. One of my Albanian patients told me recently that this is still the case. However, an orange-flavoured liqueur, which may have been called '*portokali*', and a palatable Albanian brandy, named '*Skanderbeg*' after Albania's greatest hero, compensated for the lack of potable wine. And, Turkish coffee was always readily available to round off a meal.

Gjirokastër is the birthplace of Albania's dictator Enver Hoxha. He was born there in 1908, son of bourgeois parents. His family home, which was a far less modest dwelling than many others in the town, had been converted into a museum. It was filled with traditional folkloric Albanian artefacts, and was pleasurable to explore. After our group had visited this place, I decided to spend a little time on my own, taking photographs of the many fine examples of dwellings which were built the style, which can be observed throughout the Balkans and also in Turkey. Whilst I wandered up and down the steep streets of the old city, occasional people watched me curiously, and some made friendly gestures, but no one was bold enough to risk engaging me in conversation.

Somewhere in Albania, and it might have been in Gjirokastër, I was standing with some of our group in a square when an Albanian approached us. Just as he began to speak to us, someone standing close by pulled him away from us. I have since learnt that communicating with foreigners was a dangerous pursuit that might lead a person into having to spend a long time in prison.

Whilst I was enjoying Gjirokastër's small lanes, most of the rest of our group had gone off to visit the city's fortress. After they had returned and I rejoined them, I realised that I had missed a real treat. This was not the fine view of the city that the fortress afforded, but something that was displayed in one of its courtyards. My travelling companions had been shown a small aeroplane, which was said to be an American (US) spy-plane that had been brought down by the Albanians. I would have loved to have seen that. It was a souvenir of one of several abortive attempts of the Western Powers to rescue the Albanians from Communist 'oppression' in the 1950s and before. An early plan, known as "*Valuable Project*" by the British and "*Fiend*" by the US, to stir up a revolt against Hoxha's regime foundered because secret plans relating to this were leaked to the Russians, who were at that time Albania's allies, by the British double-agent 'Kim' Philby.

I discovered recently that one of the Albanian participants in a plot to topple Hoxha's regime in the 1950s was a cousin of Mehmet Shehu. Shehu, who has been quoted as saying in public *"Whoever disagrees with our leadership in any respect, will get spat in the face, punched on the chin, and, if necessary, a bullet in his head"*, was Hoxha's hard-line right hand man. Sadly for him, he fell foul of Hoxha by expressing disagreement with his leader's isolationist approach, and ended up with a bullet in his own head a year or two before I visited Albania. His mysterious ending has been recorded in a novel, *"The Successor"* by Ismail Kadare, who was also born in Gjirokastër and has been nominated for a Nobel Prize for Literature several times.

We might have been informed whilst we were in Gjirokastër that Kadare had been born there, but I don't remember hearing that. By 1984, although world famous, Ismail Kadare was fading out of the regime's favour. In 1990, he was given political asylum in France. However, I was able to purchase an Albanian-published English translation of his early novel *"The General of the Dead Army"* (1963) in one of the many bookshops that I visited on our tour. Although I have read many of Kadare's excellent novels, I have yet to read the one, which I bought in his native land.

Gjirokastër, 1927

That evening after dinner, a number of us sat with Aferdita and Eduart in the hotel's night club. Each of the hotels in which we stayed had one of these. With the exception of our two guides and the musicians who performed in them, these clubs were out-of-bounds for Albanians. This evening we were entertained by a small band that played western pop music, mainly tunes originally performed by the Beatles. The noisy background of these clubs provided our two young guides with opportunities to ask us about life beyond their country's tightly sealed borders. However, it was clear that Aferdita was trying to eavesdrop on Eduart and vice-versa. As the musicians strummed away in the semi-gloom of the club in Gjirokastër, Aferdita turned to me, rolled her lower lip away from her teeth, and asked my opinion of her gums. She wanted to know if they had been treated properly. I told her that I was unable to give her an opinion in such poor light.

The following morning, I spotted some tubes of Albanian toothpaste on display in a locked glass display case near the hotel's main entrance. I tried to communicate to the receptionist (who did not understand English) that I wished to purchase a tube. I used to collect toothpastes from wherever I travelled, and was curious to taste its contents. Whilst I was doing this, Aferdita appeared, and asked me what I wanted. I told her. She explained my desire to the receptionist, and moments later I had become the proud owner of a tube of Albanian dentifrice.

Our next stopping place was Berat. The modern centre of the town, where a large open-air bus-station and our hotel were located, lay on flat terrain beside a river. Rows of houses were piled, seemingly on top of each other, on the slopes of the hillsides of the valley in which the town lay. From the lowest part of the town, where our hotel stood, the windows of these typical Balkan houses stared out across the valley like a wall of eyes. The Albanians call Berat "*The City of a Thousand Windows*" and also "*një mbi një*" meaning 'one over another' - a reference to the apparent stacking of these houses, one above the other. In any case, the resulting effect was that these dwellings gave the town a most attractive appearance.

After eating lunch, we were taken in our coach to a viewpoint high above the town. Whilst we were enjoying the panorama, Karen, a British archaeologist who lived in Athens, pointed out a building far below us in a part of the town across the river. It was clear to her and most of us who were looking at it, that this was, or must once have been, a church.

"Impossible," declared Aferdita, our Albanian guide, when we pointed this out to her. "There are no churches in Albania."

A few moments later, we heard distant bells ringing, and saw a small group of people leaving the building. When we suggested to Aferdita that these might possibly have been worshippers, she hurried us back into our waiting coach.

Next morning whilst I was eating breakfast, I was certain that a man, who was not a member of our party, was watching me. He appeared to be reading a newspaper, but whenever I looked at him out of the corner of my eye, I saw that he was peering in my direction over the top of his paper. His behaviour was the stuff of spy stories. When I had finished eating, I left the hotel to investigate a small lane lined with shops. It was overshadowed by a huge statue of Enver Hoxha. I noticed that the man with the newspaper was following me. When I reached the end of the short stretch of stalls, I turned around abruptly and began retracing my steps. Our eyes met for an instant as I walked past him. He knew that I was aware of what he was up to, but that did not stop him from tailing me. I don't know what he made of me when I stopped at one of the little shops, and then purchased two short-sleeved checked cotton shirts, which were manufactured in Albania. I wore these for many years, abandoning them only when I outgrew them. However, I refuse to let anyone else wear them (my teenage daughter coveted them many years later) or to throw them away. They are precious souvenirs of my unusual experience in Berat.

Although the distance between Berat and the southern coastal town of Sarandë is not great, it took many hours of driving to reach it on the roads that wound across the ridges of mountains that comprise much of the country.

Sarandë lies on the shores of a bay that opens out into the Adriatic Sea. In many ways it was a typical lazy looking Mediterranean seaside town, albeit rarely visited by holidaymakers from outside Albania. It is situated close to the north-western border of Greece, the wild part of that country in which was located the village described in John Gage's fascinating, but heartrending, novel "*Eleni*". The name 'Sarandë' resembles '$\sigma\alpha\rho\acute\alpha\nu\tau\alpha$' the Greek word for 'forty'. The Italians used to call the place '*Santi Quaranta*' ('forty saints') in honour of 40 Christian martyrs, but by the time we reached the place, these poor unfortunates were not officially recognised by the Hoxha regime. Neither was the mosque, which we stumbled upon quite by chance. It had not been demolished, but instead it had been hidden from view by surrounding it by crudely built blocks of flats made of unadorned brickwork.

Now, here we were in Sarandë, just across the short stretch of sea separating Albania from Corfu. I learnt that there were soldiers in the hills surrounding the port. They were equipped, as I was when I visited Corfu many years earlier, with high performance binoculars. They used these to detect anyone bold enough to attempt to leave Albania and also those who were foolhardy enough to stray into its territorial waters. I had read occasional reports of the fate of those who did enter Albanian by mistake. If they were intercepted by the powerful speed boats that patrolled the coast, they were held, often for a long time, in Albania's horrific penal system.

During the two days we spent in Sarandë, we were taken on an interesting excursion. We drove south to Butrint, where one of Albania's most important archaeological sites is located. After exploring the extensive Greco-Roman ruins, I stood on a raised piece of land overlooking a narrow plain that stretched away to the south. Across the narrow plain there were some low hills, no more than 3 miles away. Some of these were in Greece. To my right, was the part of the Albanian coast, that which I believed that I had viewed from Corfu so many years before.

Somewhere near Butrint, Karen's mother, who was travelling with us, picked a small yellow flower that was growing wild on the ground and showed it to our guide Aferdita, saying:

"Do you know what kind of flower this is, dear?"

"I am sorry, I don't know."

"Well, I saw something just like this growing in Sicily."

Aferdita turned on the elderly lady, and declared:

"Impossible: that is Albanian flower."

This incident puzzled me for a while. Years later, I wondered whether Karen's mother's interest in wild flowers had reminded Aferdita of something that she might have been told about Margaret Hasluck, the anthropologist who wrote an authoritative book in English about the Law of Lek. Lek Dukagjini (1410–1481) was an Albanian prince, a contemporary of Skanderbeg, Albania's greatest hero. His greatest legacy was his '*Kanun*' - a series of laws governing the tribes who inhabit the north of Albania. It includes the codification of the complicated rules, which must be obeyed when feuding tribes are conducting a vendetta. During the Second World War, Hasluck was recruited by the British SOE and advised the Allies on the situation in Albania. She was frowned upon by Enver Hoxha, who regarded her as one of his regime's earliest detractors. Whether or not she, like Karen's mother and many other English ladies of a certain age, was actually interested in wild flowers, I have no idea, but I consider it likely. I believe that Aferdita might have also been taught to think along these lines, and therefore interpreted Karen's mother's question as being a challenge to Albania's superiority.

We had a late lunch at Ksamil in an establishment, which was either a model collective farm or a worker's holiday resort - I cannot remember which. The meal, which we were served there on an open-air terrace overlooking the sea, was the only time when we were served fish. I suspect that off-shore fishing was not encouraged as it might have provided an easy route for those wishing to escape from Albania. From a vantage point near the terrace, I could see the coastline of Corfu shimmering in the heat haze. There, one could gaze at the 'free' world. It was so near, yet so far.

Ksamil is located on a thin strip of land which separates the Adriatic from a lagoon almost completely surrounded by land. As we drove around the inland stretch of water on our way back to Sarandë, we saw wooden frames with strings hanging down into the water. We were informed that these were mussel farms.

Back in Sarandë, one of our group noticed that all of the television aerials were pointing to the west, towards Italy rather than Tirana. Doubtless, they could receive broadcasts from Italian stations. I often wonder what comparisons the illicit users of these aerials made of the life outside isolationist Albania - especially the version portrayed on Italian programmes. By viewing Italian, or any other foreign broadcasts, ordinary Albanians would have put themselves at risk from getting into considerable trouble with the authorities.

Our unpredictable itinerary took us inland from Sarandë, and northward. Whilst driving through the mountains towards Durrës, one of Albania's two principal sea ports (the other being Vlorë, which we were not allowed to visit as it was an important naval base: one much coveted by both the Russians and the Chinese), we passed a sign to a village, whose name Karen recognised. She knew that it was inhabited by members of Albania's tiny Greek speaking community. She asked the driver to stop, which he did.

With some reluctance, Julian and his Albanian colleagues, Eduart and Aferdita, allowed the driver to take us off the main road and along the rough track leading into the centre of the village. The buildings in the village, which differed little in appearance from other small places, which we had passed, were plastered with political slogans in Greek rather than Albanian. Karen translated some of them for us. On arrival in the village, the driver made a u-turn and returned towards the main road without stopping. I doubt that many of those who were travelling with me realised that we had just glimpsed something which the Albanians were not keen to show us. I noticed that the two men, who admitted that they were only visiting the country as part of their attempt to visit every nation on the map, were fast asleep. Some days later, Karen pointed out to me a copy of a Greek version of the Albania's only state newspaper *Zeri I Popullit* lying on a table in the lobby of a hotel.

Appolonia, 1957

Our next stopping place was the archaeological site of Appolonia. We visited the well-preserved amphitheatre and other monuments there before driving through the town of Fier. Somewhere in the environs of that town we passed a sight that reminded me of pictures of Texas during the early days of the oil industry. For a few miles, we drove through a hilly area dotted with oil derricks and nodding donkeys, which were lazily pumping out Albania's once much sought-after oil from beneath the ground. We encountered the occasional tanker trucks on the road. Eduart became most concerned when Maynard, next to whom he sitting at the rear of the coach, declared that the trucks were empty.

"How do you know?" he asked, alarmed.

"That's simple," Maynard replied, grinning. "If they were full, the weight of the oil would have deformed the tyres."

The Hotel Adriatik, located in a grove of trees just south of Durrës, was under restoration when we arrived there in the early afternoon. This was where our Regents Holiday itinerary had promised that we would have spent two nights by the sea, but one quick look at the place provided a possible explanation for our altered programme. A group of us walked the short distance from the Adriatik into the town, passing the larger than usual dome-shaped concrete bunkers, which punctuated the coastline every few yards.

The enormous Roman amphitheatre in Durrës was well-preserved. Our local guide showed us an entrance almost hidden within the rows of seats. This led to a small early Christian chapel decorated with coloured mosaics. The contents of the museum, which was located near to the amphitheatre, seemed to me just like any other archaeological collection. It was filled with sculptures, some of which, we were informed, were Greek and others Roman. After we had left the building, Karen, who was trained as an archaeologist, told me that all was not as it had seemed within the museum. She had noticed that some of the exhibits were hybrids: Roman heads had been carefully and seamlessly attached to Greek bodies and vice-versa. We walked towards the city's seashore. When we arrived there, and began strolling along the promenade lined with palm trees, Karen's mother announced that the place felt uncannily familiar. Then, she remembered why. She had visited Durrës sometime before the Second World War during her childhood whilst on an Adriatic cruise with her parents.

Durrës, 1957

That night and the following were spent at the Tirana Hotel in the capital. This yet again unpredicted stay in Tirana annoyed some of our party, but was full of interest for me. We visited

"*Shqiperia Sot*" (i.e. 'Albania Today'). Housed in a large hangar-like building, this was an exhibition of Albania's technical achievements. These included a tractor manufactured in Albania. The ever perceptive Maynard pointed out that although it differed in design from the Chinese tractors that we had seen on our travels, we had not seen even one of these home-made machines anywhere outside the exhibition. My favourite exhibit was under glass in a showcase containing Albanian toys. It was a yellow plastic bunny rabbit holding a rifle in exactly the same pose as the soldier, who had watched our arrival at the Albanian frontier. Even as infants, Albanians needed constant reminding of the need to defend their country. I would have loved to have purchased one of these militant bunnies, but I saw none for sale anywhere. It is my contention that the items exhibited were made especially for the exhibition, and not widely available, if at all.

There was what appeared to be a major department store near to our hotel. I decided to investigate it. After passing through the double doors at its entrance I came face to face with a huge pyramid made by balancing rows of cardboard boxes on top of each other. Each box contained a pearl light bulb. On closer examination, I discovered that these were imports from Hungary. I did not venture further into the store, mainly because it was very poorly lit. Instead, I spent an enjoyable time wandering around the city's streets.

After passing a shop window in which there was a display of elaborately decorated cakes for special occasions, I discovered a bookshop. I bought several volumes of the collected writings of Enver Hoxha (in English), a book about earthquakes in Albania during 1979, and books on a variety of other topics - some in English, others in Albanian. Amongst these were a two volume Albanian and English dictionary and a phrasebook for tourists written using extremely picturesque English. Laden with my purchases I continued my ramblings. I chanced upon two elderly ladies dressed in traditional costumes. They were lurking in a quiet side street, furtively trying to sell small bunches of what must have been herbs. This was the only evidence of private enterprise that I saw in Albania.

A huge rectangular mosaic adorned the façade of the National Historical Museum of Albania, a modern building in the centre of the city. It shows a number of people holding a huge red flag. I was told that amongst the faces depicted on it there was one of the recently deceased, and, by now, much discredited Mehmet Shehu. Unlike many of the photographs, which we had seen in various museums, which contained faces that had been made unidentifiable by covering them with black ink, no one had found a way of removing Shehu's portrait from this mosaic without completely wrecking its appearance.

After we had eaten lunch at the hotel, a group of us went into the square outside it. We saw a long line of taxis, which were waiting vacantly by a booking booth. We wondered how often these were hired and by whom; there was not a soul in sight taking the slightest interest in them. One of us walked up to the booth and asked the man sitting inside whether we could hire a taxi to take us up to Mount Dajti, some way outside Tirana. Just when it seemed that we had succeeded in hiring a cab, another person inside the booth lifted a telephone receiver, listened for a moment, and then whispered something to the man with whom we had just negotiated. He beckoned to us, and pointed at the hotel. Somehow, he made it clear to us that we needed to book the taxi not from him, but from the hotel reception desk.

We trooped back into the hotel's lobby and made a beeline for the reception desk. Two suited men, sitting on a sofa nearby, looked at us over the tops of their newspapers. As we reached the desk, I noticed that the doors of one of the hotel's two lifts were opening. Our Eduart hurried through them and towards the receptionist, who was beginning to attend to us.

"What do you need?" Eduart asked us, out of breath.

"We want to hire a taxi."

"Why?"

"We want to visit Mount Dajti?"

"Why should you do that?"

"We need some fresh country air. We've been in the city for too long."

"That's ridiculous," Eduart protested. "You have already spent many days in the countryside."

"But, that's what we want, and we believe that the views from Mount Dajti are magnificent."

"You cannot go."

"Why ever not?" we asked.

"There is a lot of traffic. The roads are crowded."

We looked at Eduart disbelievingly. Traffic congestion was certainly not a problem in Albania in 1984.

"You know that there's a big national cycle race on at the moment."

"That was over long ago," one of us objected. "We saw the posters announcing it along the roads."

"You can visit Mother Albania, but no further."

We had already visited the Mother Albania monument, which was located in the outskirts of the town. However, as we were determined to not to give in to our obstreperous guide, we agreed to his compromise.

"Alright," we said.

Then, Eduart said menacingly:

"You may take the taxi to Mother Albania, but remember that if anything happens to you, we cannot take any responsibility for your safety. You will not be protected by your group visa."

"We'll risk it," one of us said.

I did not like the threatening sound of Eduart's voice, but followed the rest of our small group back to the taxi rank. When we arrived there no more that ten minutes after we had left it, we found that all of the taxis had disappeared, and also there was an extremely long line of people waiting in a queue outside the booth. Accepting defeat, we made our way on foot to a park, which contained Tirana's zoological gardens. The only animals that I remember seeing were a few wolves. They were sitting in a cage, and were looking as dejected as we felt after our recent encounter with Eduart.

After dinner at the Tirana Hotel, a number of us who did not feel like spending yet another evening in a hotel's night club, wandered down the wide avenue, which led from Skanderbeg Square towards the university. Soon, we reached the Hotel Dajti. This elegant hotel had been built by the Italians in the 1930s, and the part of its interior that we were able to see had retained its original stylish appearance. Almost as soon as we set foot into the hotel, we were ushered down some stairs into the basement. A ball was in progress. All of the dancers were elegantly dressed. The women were wearing ball-gowns, and the men tuxedos. They all danced most gracefully. It felt as if we had been thrust into the midst of the New Years Eve Ball in Vienna. I suspect that we had intruded on a ball organised by Tirana's diplomatic community. Many years later, my step-mother, who had lived in Tirana as a member of the Greek diplomatic corps, told me that there were sparingly few ways of spending a diverting evening in Enver Hoxha's Tirana. Attending balls must have been one of these.

We left Tirana, and drove inland towards the city of Elbasan, an industrial town in the centre of a metal ore mining district. I remember little about the place except that its brown chimneys and steelworks (built with Chinese assistance as was the wire factory at Shkodër) were visible long before we arrived there. We only stopped in the city for a short time, but it was long enough for us to discover a well-hidden, largish orthodox Christian basilica, which seemed quite old. Sadly, we did not have sufficient time to examine it properly. The next part of our journey took us through mountainous territory. The winding road, along which we drove, kept crossing an equally sinuous railway track until we arrived at Lin, a village on the shore of Lake Ohrid, the expanse of water shared with Yugoslavia.

Elbasan, 1927

We stopped for lunch at an unattractive hotel by the lakeside at Pogradec. Compared to the towns that I had visited on the Yugoslav shore on the lake, this small resort was disappointing; it was neither particularly picturesque nor interesting. However, the shore of Yugoslavia, from which I had gazed at Albania in the past, was just about discernible through the heat haze. After eating, we continued our journey towards Korçë our next destination.

After a while, we passed a field in the middle of which there was an old, attractive, isolated, Orthodox basilica built of reddish brick. It was about 50 to 100 yards from the edge of the road. Some of our party yelled to the driver asking him to stop. He did. Several people got out of their seats and pushed towards the front of the coach, demanding to be allowed to disembark. Our driver opened the door, and they did. As soon as they were out on the road, they began running through the stubble towards the church in order to explore it. This made Julian become agitated.

71

"This is not allowed. No one said that they could go over there," he shouted.

"But, they only want to take a closer look at that old church," someone protested.

This infuriated Julian even more.

"Start the coach," he shouted to the driver, before adding in a nasty tone of voice: "We'll continue without them, and then let them see how they get on without the group visa."

To my great surprise and disbelief, the driver started the coach's motor, revved it noisily, and then drove forward and around the corner of the field in which the church stood. Selfishly, I felt relieved that I had decided - only heaven knows why - not to join the adventurous explorers. I looked out of the window. The churchgoing party did not appear concerned about our leaving them behind. And, they need not have been because the driver stopped the bus after we had rounded the corner. When the 'miscreants' had re-embarked, Julian told them off soundly. He seemed to have forgotten that we were all adults and that he was supposed to be working on our behalf. During this curious affair, neither of our two Albanian guides nor the driver intervened. They observed silently.

We reached Korçë in the late afternoon, and settled into our hotel, which was located on one side of a triangular open space in the city's centre. Like everywhere else in Albania, it was devoid of motorised traffic. Our bedroom's windows looked over this 'square' towards a building, which was a perfect example of the style of public architecture that was favoured by the Italian Fascist authorities in the 1930s. It was the city's branch of the National Bank of Albania. Some of the banks in other Albanian towns, which we visited, were built in this style, most probably by the Italians whilst they held sway over the country.

The next morning, I walked over to the bank to cash a traveller's cheque. I showed my passport to a teller, who wrote down my name as being '*Adam Robert*'. As was the case everywhere in Albania, he did not copy down my actual surname. This may have been because my surname '*Yamey*' was written on a line below the one showing given names. I took the documents, which the teller had prepared, to the cashier. He was seated inside a large barred metal cage. A high wall made of brick-like wads of Albanian banknotes lined the inside of his cage and almost surrounded him. He dealt with his customers through a small hatch in his lattice-work enclosure. However, this was big enough for anyone to reach inside to help themselves to a brick or two of Albanian Leks, each of them easily worth several hundred pounds (Sterling). I resisted the temptation! I imagine that high security was hardly necessary in a bank in such a vigilant country as Albania.

Korçë, more than any other town in Albania, looked like a well-established provincial city - almost central European in character - even though it was devoid of traffic and a 'buzz' of activity. I must digress to mention that although Albania seemed a very quiet place, it felt nowhere as quiet as Bulgaria, which I had visited one year earlier. Many of the Korçë's buildings were well-built, attractively designed, and dated back to the 19th century. I would have liked to have lingered for several days in this little place, which was coveted by Greece during most of the 20th century, but we were only there for one night.

We were driven past a bazaar, all of whose single-storied shops were closed, tightly secured with rusty metal shutters. Soon, we reached a large, heavily-guarded building, which was opened up especially for our group. It contained a museum consisting of several rooms whose walls were covered with religious paintings. We were shown around this collection of valuable artwork by a scholarly-looking gentleman, whom I understood to be the curator and also an historian of art. A number of us asked him questions. Aferdita translated them into Albanian for him.

Whenever anyone asked him about the biblical subjects portrayed, he seemed unable, or, more likely, reluctant to provide an answer. I suspect that he thought that it would be best for his safety if he appeared to Aferdita and Eduart, who for all he knew may have been working for the Sigurimi, to be ignorant of the stories from the Bible, which were depicted in most of the works of art on display.

It was a long drive from Korçë back to Tirana. We passed countless domed concrete bunkers and travelled through a landscape filled with political slogans. Some of these, which were as widely distributed throughout the country as were the bunkers, were on hoardings by the roadside. Others were spelled out in enormous letters on the slopes of hills and mountains. They could be read from a great distance. The letters forming these gigantic propaganda messages were made up of innumerable white stones painstakingly gathered together by children and other 'volunteers'. This is well illustrated in "*Slogans*", a film made by an Albanian director in 2001.

The film depicts a school in a small Albanian village during the late 1970s. The school's director has received news that an important party member is planning to visit the district. Day after day, the teachers take their young pupils out onto a mountainside and they collect stones frantically, and arrange them to create a giant political slogan. Meanwhile, other preparations are being made to welcome the dignitary. The great day finally arrives, and the villagers line up along the village street, waiting excitedly. The car carrying the celebrity is sighted in the distance. It roars right through the village at high speed without stopping. The party member being transported does not even look up from the papers that he was perusing as he was driven past the people who were awaiting his visit so eagerly.

The roadside propaganda was so successful that a number of the messages remain firmly etched in my brain. There were many slogans plastered all over the country, but little variety in the messages that they conveyed. "Work, Disciple, Vigilance" written in Albanian, was a common roadside exhortation. Many a mountainside was adorned with "*Parti Enver*" ('Party of Enver') or "*Lavdi PPSH*", which means 'Praise the PPSH' (PPSH being an abbreviation for '*Partia e Punës e Shqipërisë*' - the Albanian Workers' Party. And, the words "*Rroftë shoku Enver!*", which translates as 'Long live Comrade Enver', praised the country's only party's leader and appeared everywhere.

In 2001, long after my trip to Albania, I began working in a dental practice in west London. Many of my patients were, and still are, refugees from the places in the world, which are stricken by military and political conflicts. Algerians, Iraqis, Afghans, Kurds, Palestinians, Eritreans, and many other others who have fled their far-off disturbed homes sit in my surgery and reveal the ravages that life has inflicted on their teeth. During the terrible conflicts in the former Yugoslavia, many of my patients hailed from Kosovo, and usually spoke poor English in addition to their native Albanian. Many were the smiles that I elicited from them when I quoted the old party slogans, undoubtedly poorly pronounced, and wished them '*Mir u pafshim*' instead of 'Goodbye' at the end of their appointments.

On our way to Tirana, we stopped to make another factory visit. This time, we were not thwarted by bad weather as we were at the copper wire factory near to Shkodër. This particular factory, we were informed, produced precision scientific instruments. My overriding memory is of a large room filled with chemicals, containers of molten metal, and a variety of tools. The air inside it smelled unpleasantly acrid. Nowhere in Western Europe would such a workplace have conformed to health and safety rules, even in the relatively lax 1980s. At the end of the tour, I was allowed to examine a sliding (Vernier) calliper, which had been made in the factory. It was a crude object, whose jaw slid jerkily rather than smoothly. The markings were badly scored and looked a little irregular. I handed it back to the factory's director, and smiled politely.

When we boarded our coach after leaving the factory, Maynard, who was sitting behind me next to Eduart, said to his neighbour:

"Adam is a scientist. Let's ask his opinion of the precision instruments."

"Yes, that would be interesting," Eduart, our budding Sigurimi officer, said.

In retrospect, what I said may have been rather tactless, but it was the truth. I turned my head to the two men sitting behind me and said:

"The instrument that I was shown could not really be considered as being for precision use. It might be suitable for young schoolchildren to learn with."

Eduart's face fell, but that did not worry me as he was proving to be a less than pleasant travelling companion. He had no idea about the world beyond Albania's borders, nothing with which to compare his own self-contained world.

Maynard and Eduart spent most of the time seated together at the back of the coach. Eduart was keen to hear Maynard's opinions about Albania and world politics. In turn, it amused Maynard to pull our guide's leg with his witty interpretations of life. The two of them amused each other by telling jokes, most of them less than tasteful. One day, we asked Eduart to tell us a typically Albanian joke. There was, he began, a small bridge across a fast-running river. It was only wide enough for one car to cross at a time. Two cars travelling in opposite directions arrived at either end of the bridge. One was driven by a Frenchman, the other by an Englishman. Neither would let the other pass. They sat in their cars at either end of the bridge, glaring at each other. Eventually, the Frenchman took out a large volume and then began reading it. Many hours passed. When the Englishman saw that the Frenchman had finished the book, he walked across the bridge and knocked on his window. The Frenchman wound it down, and asked the Englishman what he wanted. The Englishman replied:

"That book, which you were reading, must have been interesting. Would you mind lending it to me?"

The Frenchman handed him the novel. The Englishman returned to his car, sat down, and began reading it.

Back in Tirana, Julian along with his Marxist fellow travellers, the young socialist couple, achieved nirvana for an hour or so. We were assembled for dinner in the hotel, which had almost become a second home for us having stayed there so often during our fortnight in Albania, when they arrived, looking jubilant. They had just visited the studios of Radio Tirana, where they had been interviewed. Doubtless, their blinkered views on Albania, had been sufficiently fulsome of the regime, which would not have allowed them as much political freedom as they were accustomed to enjoy back home, where the food did not upset their stomachs. Proudly, they displayed the metal badges bearing the Albanian flag, which the radio station had given them as rewards for whatever they had said. They had not been at the studio alone. A typically bourgeois lady, 'middle England' in attitudes and also a member of our group, had been invited along with them. She had, she admitted, expressed her praise of the hospitality that we had all received during our trip, but seemed concerned that she might have been a little hasty in doing so. She was worried lest people she knew might hear her words broadcast by a regime of which most of them would have disapproved. I think that she would have been quite safe in assuming that none of her acquaintances have ever bothered, or even considered, retuning their radios from the BBC to Radio Tirana.

Tirana, 1957

We were nearing the end of our stay in Albania. During the trip, I had bought many books, all published in Albania. I wanted to carry them back home to England, but there was a problem. I knew from what I had read before setting out for Albania that any books published in Albania were liable to confiscation by the Yugoslav customs. Albania and its Slav neighbour were on bad terms with one another. The advice, which I had received before leaving England, was that all books purchased in Albania should be posted back home. In addition, I had learnt that wrapping materials were hard to obtain in Albania. I did not check this out in Tirana because I had made sure that when I packed my rucksack I had included plenty of brown paper, sellotape, and string. I wrapped my books into a number of parcels, addressed them, and then began leaving the hotel to visit Tirana's main post office. The Australian, who was travelling with us, spotted me in the lobby and asked me what I was doing. When I told him, he asked whether he could accompany me to the post office, as he, working as he did for the Australian postal service, was curious to see how things were done by the Albanian post.

During one of my many trips to Belgrade, another place where I used to purchase many books, I bought a particularly heavy book. As I did not want to add to my already weighty baggage, I wrapped it, planning to send it by book-post. At a large post-office in central Belgrade, the official behind the counter took one look at my parcel and said that it could not be posted as it was. She sent me to a small office near the main entrance. There, a man ripped off all of my wrapping and then re-packaged my book very carefully in brown paper in such a way that the bottom fifth remained uncovered to prove that the parcel contained a book, and was therefore eligible for being sent at the cheaper 'printed matter' parcel rate.

The clerk behind the counter in the Tirana post office offered no objection to the way that I had packed my parcels. He weighed them and then gave me numerous stamps to stick on them. I stuck them on and returned the parcels one by one. The clerk examined each of them to make sure that I had stuck the right combination of stamps on each packet. Suddenly, he stopped, looked up at me, then at the parcel, before pointing at one of the stamps. In my haste, I had stuck it on upside down. He tore the stamp off the parcel, and then replaced it the right way up, pointing at the portrait on it whilst saying:

"Enver Hoxha."

The Australian, who was watching this with wide-open eyes, turned to me and said:

"You know, it's completely illegal to remove stamps from postage. It's against all international postal rules."

I did not know what to say, but admired the respect that even a humble postage stamp could inspire in one of Enver's subjects.

After bidding Tirana a final farewell, we were driven to Krujë. This was the stronghold of George Kastrioti Skanderbeg (1405 –1468), better known as 'Skanderbeg'. He was Albania's greatest warrior, and greatly revered by the Hoxha regime. His heroic actions defended the Albanians from the Ottomans for more than 20 years. The heavily restored castle at Krujë, which Skanderbeg defended from the Turks for two decades, contained a museum, which sadly I did not feel like entering. By not visiting it, I missed seeing an amazing display of monumental sculptures and other visual displays, all with stirring propagandistic subtexts. Whilst the others were exploring the museum, I wandered around the long street lined with shops selling folkloric handicrafts. This was undoubtedly aimed at the large number of Albanian visitors who were brought to Krujë to pay their respects to the country's greatest hero.

Either just before visiting Krujë or after, we visited a museum displaying contemporary Albanian art. The pieces were not exceptionally beautiful. Some sculptures were placed in the open-air on a roof terrace. They depicted figures posed to look heroic or strong. They reminded me of the work of one of my relatives, who sculpted for a hobby. Like his works, they were highly expressive but amateurishly executed.

On our way to the frontier, we stopped in Shkodër, either for a few hours or overnight. I cannot remember which. It was during the last few hours of our stay in Albania that I managed finally to take a good photograph of a horse-drawn truck. I had tried in vain to capture one of these on film from the windows of our moving bus, but I was never quick enough. I remember taking this picture in Shkodër whilst one of my companions was talking about the Sigurimi.

We returned to the border post where we had entered Albania a fortnight earlier. Of the few formalities there, only one was memorable. As we disembarked from our coach for the last time, each passenger, who had been required to surrender the tourist brochure from Montenegro that contained the picture of a nudist beach, was reunited with his or her brochure. We bade farewell to our three Albanian 'minders' and walked across the frontier to the Yugoslav border post.

I sat next to the Australian postal worker on the flight back to London. He told me that Aferdita had become very friendly with him. She had even invited him to a flat in Tirana - it might have been hers, but he was not sure about that. She had tried unsuccessfully, so he told me, to seduce him. On another

80

occasion, she and Eduart approached him to try to recruit him to carry out espionage on Australia for Albania. He had the impression that whoever was instructing our two guides, believed that working for the post-office was a cover-up for a more sensitive job, which gave him access to Australian military information. It puzzled me what use Albania, being so far from Australia, would have had for such secrets.

The Albanians might not have learnt much from the Australian postman, but the reverse was true. He confided in me that a number of us had been regarded by the Albanian authorities as being highly suspicious, and therefore worthy of close observation. The woman with the American accent was one of these. Despite travelling with a British passport, she was American nevertheless. And, the USA was one of Albania's greatest enemies. Karen, the archaeologist had also been closely observed. She lived and worked in Athens, spoke Greek, and seemed to be well-informed about Albania. They must have wondered whether she was a Greek agent. In 1984, Greece and Albania were still technically at war, although not much had happened for several decades. The Albanians were most suspicious about Jerry, my room mate. According to my Australian informant, they knew that Jerry's wife was a Romanian, and that she was in Romania. Maybe they had thought that Ceaucescu's secret police had sent Jerry to spy on Albania whilst they held his wife hostage in Romania. I doubted that was the case, but as Jerry did make telephone calls to his wife from Albania they might well have thought that they had some grounds for their suspicions.

My Australian neighbour on the aeroplane told me about one other thing, of which I had been unaware whilst we were touring around Albania. Many of my companions on the trip had found that their cameras had been tampered with. Film had been torn out of cameras left in bedrooms. This did not happen to me because I carried my pocket-sized Olympus 35 mm camera around with me all the time. I had bought it especially for the trip because of its small size and great portability. However, I was surprised that I had not heard anyone complaining about this problem on the trip. Had one of my films been removed, I am sure that I would have kicked up a fuss.

After we had collected our baggage at London's Heathrow Airport and before we all went our separate ways, we spent a few minutes saying farewell and exchanging addresses. It was during these last moments together that people began to reveal their real professions. A middle-aged lady, with whom I had enjoyed discussing things, turned out to be the editorial secretary of the *New Statesman*. Maynard, who had never disclosed his profession, revealed that he wrote reports for business intelligence digest. And Karen, who had convinced me by her learned comments that she was a professional archaeologist, revealed that she was not only that but also a journalist for "*The Athenian*", the Greek edition of the better-known American weekly, the "*New Yorker*". I have no idea whether the Albanians, who forbade the entry of foreign journalists to their country unless specially invited, were aware that these journalists had accompanied us on our tour.

I returned to my home in Gillingham (Kent), pleased that I had made it at last to the country, which had obsessed me for so long. Not only had the visit surpassed all of my expectations, but also it had been so enjoyable. Almost everyone on the tour was good company and most of them highly interesting to converse with. I returned to work, and my books arrived safely from Albania a few weeks later.

Epilogue

I have wanted to set down my fading memories of my trip to Albania for some time. What finally prompted be to get on with writing them was a brief conversation I had with a dental patient whose surname is Hoxha. He was a little younger than me, but old enough to remember what life was like living in Enver Hoxha's Albania. After I had related a number of anecdotes about my trip, he turned to me and said:

"You must write these things down. No one believes me when I tell about how terrible it was living in Albania in those times, but they will believe you, an observer from the outside world."

I hope that I have not stretched your credulity beyond reasonable limits.

TWO VAGABONDS IN ALBANIA
By JAN GORDON and CORA J. GORDON with Illustrations by the Authors

LONDON: JOHN LANE THE BODLEY HEAD LIMITED
NEW YORK: DODD, MEAD AND COMPANY

Some books on Albania

This brief annotated bibliography contains some of the books on Albania, which I have found enjoyable. It is by no means comprehensive. I have arranged them in order of date of publication.

Lear, E,: "Journals of a Landscape Painter in Albania etc.", publ. Richard Bentley (London) 1851.

This may be read on the Internet, as well as in various modern reprinted editions.

Durham, M.E.: *"High Albania"*, publ. Edward Arnold (London) 1909.

Margaret Durham was an anthropologist who fell in love with the Balkans and the people living there. This book describes in great detail the history and anthropology of the tribes living in the remote mountains of northern Albania. There are modern editions of this beautifully written and illustrated classic available.

Peacock, W.: *"Albania: The Foundling State of Europe"*, publ. Chapman & Hall (London), 1914.

This is a fascinating, detailed account of life in and around Shkodër during the first years of Albanian independence. The author was attached to the British Consulate in Shkodër. His chapter on the future of Albania makes for interesting reading in the light of what actually happened.

Gordon, J & Gordon, C.: *"Two vagabonds in Albania"*, publ. John Lane The Bodley Head (London), 1927.

Jan and Cora Gordon wrote a large number of *"Two Vagabonds in..."* travelogues. This one, which describes their trip to Albania, is beautifully illustrated with the authors' line drawings and chalk sketches. The text is humorous and informative.

Bridge, A.: *"Singing Waters"*, publ. Macmillan (New York), 1946.

Not quite as good as Bridge's *"Illyrian Spring"*, her superb novel set in the Balkans, *"Singing Waters"* is set largely in Albania.

Muggeridge, M. (ed.): *"Ciano's Diary: 1939 -1943"*, publ. William Heinemann (London), 1947.

This is a translation of Count Ciano's secret diary, which was smuggled out of Italy by Ciano's wife at the end of WW2. According to Mosely, who wrote a biography of Ciano, this is a largely accurate account of the events described in the diary. The first chapter of the diary describes the events leading up to the Italian invasion of Albania.

Amery, J.: *"Sons of the Eagle"*, publ. Macmillan (London), 1948.

Julian Amery, a right-wing British politician, described King Zog as, *"the cleverest man I have ever met."* His profusely illustrated book describes the non-communist partisans' struggle to liberate Albania during WW2 and his involvement with this. He described the young Enver Hoxha as being, *"... possessed of rare organising ability."*

Buda, A., Cun, J., Rrok, Z., & Skënder, A.: *"Guide d'Albanie"*, publ. by Editions "Albturist" (Tirana), 1958.

Difficult to obtain, this guide, produced whilst the Albanians were still allies of the Soviet Union, is remarkably detailed. The historical section ends with an affirmation of the country's alliance with the Soviet Union, '*... le grand sauveur et défenseur de notre people."*

Hamm, H.: *"Albania - China's beachhead in Europe"*, publ. Weidenfeld & Nicolson (London), 1963.

Harry Hamm was a German journalist who was allowed to visit Albania in 1962. He was the first western journalist to visit the country since 1957. He arrived just after the Albanians had divorced themselves from the Soviet Union. He describes this break up between former allies in great detail. He also foretells the alliance of Albania and the People's Republic of China, which began soon after his visit. Hard to find, this is a fascinating book.

Logoreci, A.: *"The Albanians"*, publ. Westview Press (Colorado), 1977.

Published just after the death of Mao Tse Tung, this scholarly but readable book gives many interesting insights about the political, social, and economic conditions prevailing in Hoxha's Albania. He predicts the rift that developed between China and Albania not long after Mao's death. The book ends with a comprehensive reading list over five pages in length.

Kadare, I.: "*Broken April*". First published in 1978, numerous editions are available.

This haunting tale, which revolves around the Law of Lek, the codification of feuding in traditional Albania, is a brief but brilliant story about the last days of a young man expecting to be killed in an inter-familial vendetta. As in his other works, Ismail Kadare captures a great amount of detail with remarkably few words.

Ward, P.: "*Albania*", publ. Oleander Press (Cambridge), 1983.

The author describes his trip to Albania and uses it as the framework for his informative illustrated guidebook. It is the most interesting guidebook to the country that I have come across.

Halliday, J.: "*The Artful Albanian*", publ. Chatto & Windus, 1986.

This book contains a large number of extracts from the voluminous writings of Enver Hoxha and interesting commentaries about them. The author uses these as a framework for his description of Hoxha's career. I lent my copy to one of the people with whom I travelled to Albania, and she never returned it. If she is reading this now, I would like her to return it immediately!

Robyns, G.: "*Geraldine of the Albanians: The Authorised Biography*", publ. Frederick Muller Ltd, 1987.

This true-life Mills and Boon tale, a biography of King Zog's Hungarian wife, was written by Barbara Cartland's biographer. It includes a description of Geraldine whimpering into her pillow on being deflowered.

Jones, L.: "*Biografi*", publ. André Deutsch, 1993.

This curious tale about the fate of one of Enver Hoxha's doubles or 'look-alikes' in post-communist Albania contains good descriptions of conditions in the country soon after the end of communist rule.

Pettifer, J.: "*Blue Guide: Albania*", publ. A&C Black (London), 1994.

Published soon after Albania shed its communist regime, this detailed guidebook does its best in his section on 'Personal Security' to portray Albania as a lawless place, to which only the foolhardy visitor should stray. This book provides an encyclopaedic account of Albania and her people.

Mosely, R.: *"Mussolini's Shadow"*, publ. Yale University Press (New Haven), 1999.

This detailed biography of Count Ciano, Mussolini's foreign minister and son-in-law contains a chapter on the Italian involvement in Albania during WW2.

Kadare, I.: *"The Successor"*, published in 2003.

This chilling tale, which explores the mysterious death of the successor to a political leader, is most probably based on the sudden death of Enver Hoxha's right hand man and probable successor Mehmet Shehu.

Tomes, J.: *"King Zog: Self-made monarch of Albania"*, publ. Sutton (Stroud, Gloucestershire), 2003.

This well-written, interestingly detailed account of Zog's life in Albania, and then later in exile, includes a chapter about the Western Allies attempts to wrest Albania from the Communists in the 1950s.

Kadare, I.: *"The Accident: a novel"*, first published in 2009.

This recent novel by world famous author Ismail Kadare concerns the investigation of a mysterious traffic accident near to Vienna's airport. This story does not make for easy reading. It is deliberately confusing. I suspect that it is supposed to give the reader a good insight into the tortuous thought processes that were needed to survive in the oppressive atmosphere that was inspired by Albania's long serving dictator Enver Hoxha.

Note on the illustrations

I hope that I have not infringed any existing copyright by copying: the picture dated 1909 from Durham's book, those dated 1914 from Wadham Peacock's book, those dated 1927 from Jan & Cora Gordon's book, and those dated 1957 from the Albturist guide to Albania. Other illustrations are my own.

92

Printed in Great Britain
by Amazon.co.uk, Ltd.,
Marston Gate.